Elements
of Taste

Elements
of Taste

UNDERSTANDING WHAT WE LIKE AND WHY

• • •

BENJAMIN ERRETT

A TarcherPerigee Book

tarcherperigee

An imprint of Penguin Random House LLC
375 Hudson Street
New York, New York 10014

Illustrations © Sarah Lazarovic

Most TarcherPerigee books are available at special quantity discounts for
bulk purchase for sales promotions, premiums, fund-raising, and educational needs.
Special books or book excerpts also can be created to fit specific needs.
For details, write: SpecialMarkets@penguinrandomhouse.com.

Library of Congress Cataloging-in-Publication Data
Names: Errett, Benjamin, 1978– author.
Title: Elements of taste : understanding what we like and why / Benjamin Errett.
Description: New York, NY : TarcherPerigee, [2017] | Includes bibliographical
references and index.
Identifiers: LCCN 2017020329 (print) | LCCN 2017027224 (ebook) |
ISBN 9780399183454 | ISBN 9780399183447 (alk. paper)
Subjects: LCSH: Popular culture. | Aesthetics. | Taste. | Civilization,
Modern—21st century.
Classification: LCC HM621 (ebook) | LCC HM621 E749 2017 (print) |
DDC 306—dc23
LC record available at https://lccn.loc.gov/2017020329

Printed in the United States of America
1   3   5   7   9   10   8   6   4   2

Book design by Elke Sigal

For Sarah, Plum, and Teddy

CONTENTS

Nothing classifies somebody more
than the way he or she classifies.

—PIERRE BOURDIEU

Aperitif

Ketchup Is the Perfect Food

Not nutritionally, of course. A steady diet of nothing but red sauce would destroy you in a matter of months. But when it comes to taste, very few foods hit all the notes the way ketchup does.

Let Malcolm Gladwell explain: "The taste of Heinz's ketchup began at the tip of the tongue, where our receptors for sweet and salty first appear, moved along the sides, where sour notes seem the strongest, then hit the back of the tongue, for umami and bitter, in one long crescendo."

This was in his 2004 *New Yorker* story on why Heinz ketchup has proven so difficult for competitors to challenge. The king of condiments satisfies tongues on a primal level, he concludes, coming as close to being all things to all people as is possible.

It does this through amplitude, "the word sensory experts use to describe flavors that are well blended and balanced." It's not just that all the tastes are there; it's that they're playing together like an all-star team.

If this can be done in the world of food, can it be replicated in

GENERIC
PERFECT

PERFECT

other arenas? Is there a ketchup of music, of literature, of painting, of poetry?

This book says yes, there is cultural ketchup. There is Lin-Manuel Miranda's Broadway musical *Hamilton*. There is the original *Star Wars* trilogy. There is *The Great Gatsby*. There is *Romeo and Juliet*. There is George Gershwin's "Summertime." And there are many more.

What makes these works stand out? They're popular and they're critically acclaimed, but that's not how ketchup became ketchup. It was when the key elements—red ripe tomatoes and more vinegar than seemed prudent—were finally mixed in perfect harmony. The ketchup secret was in the ingredients. To understand cultural ketchup, we have to look at the recipe. How do we get to the sweet, sour, salty, bitter, and umami of culture? We define the Elements of Taste.

When we do this, we discover not only the recipe for cultural ketchup, but also the cultural equivalents of every other taste: miso soup, Sour Patch Kids, espresso, kelp, gelato, pork chops, kumquats, ice cream. And from there, we can examine our entertainment diets from a new perspective, learning new ways to identify and satisfy cravings.

Not everyone likes *Star Wars*. Some prefer to dip their fries in mayonnaise. To those people we say, dip away. This book won't tell you what to like. No book, algorithm, or person can reliably do that, and frankly it's presumptuous to even try. Instead, it aims to help you think fondly about what you already love—and then offers a new framework to consider why you feel that way. And once you get an inkling of the reasons behind your passions, you can explore a new universe of songs, books, shows, and movies worthy of your love. Let's begin by turning on the radio.

Is there a ketchup of music, of literature, of painting, of poetry?

1

Setting the Table: How All Taste Comes Back to the Tongue

What Sort of Music Do You Like?
And How Useless Is That Question?

It's a first-date icebreaker that sounds like something a computer would ask. Instead of getting at your innate attraction to harmony, it focuses on outdated categories. No one lingers in the car after pulling into the driveway because they need to finish a genre of music. It's just not what moves us.

Or as Shirley Bassey and the Propellerheads put it in the song "History Repeating": "Some people won't dance if they don't know who's singing. Why ask your head? It's your hips that are swinging."

So how do you find out what makes your hips swing?

This was a professional dilemma for David Greenberg, a psychology researcher at the University of Cambridge who set out to determine how music intersects with personality and thinking. To do so, he and his colleagues had to first figure out what sort of music people like—and how to ask them in a way that might actually get at the truth.

"The issue with genre-based methods is that they're based on people's understanding of genres," he explains. "Genres are multi-faceted and broad. In the rock genre alone, you have Metallica, Joni Mitchell, Radiohead, Coldplay, and Rage Against the Machine. So someone could say, 'Hey, I really like rock music,' but that's not giving you too much information."

Not to mention that just about every artist of note working today crosses genres in some form or another. Taylor Swift went from country to pop; Kanye West from hip-hop to electronica; "Weird Al" Yankovic from polka to rock to rap to polka. Each of these musicians is a genre of their own, and if you like Taylor Swift, you'll likely follow her into whatever genre she tries next.

And then there's what we can call the Sloan effect, for the Canadian band's song "Coax Me" and its memorable lyric "It's not the band I hate, it's their fans." No matter how much you love blissing out to New Age music, you might not want to be a Person Who Loves Blissing Out to New Age Music. And what you sing in the shower may not be what you say to a Cambridge researcher.

And finally, music is everywhere. When your local news station transitions from sports to weather with a dubstep beat, you may find yourself humming along. SUV commercials are used to debut new tracks by respectable bands. Regular visits to the grocery store expose you to Adele's complete back catalog. Even if you never seek out a song, you may find that your musical preferences are much more diverse than you expected them to be.

To avoid these issues, David Greenberg used a system built around the idea that "musical preferences are based on preferences for particular musical properties and psychological attributes as opposed to musical genres."

This system, devised by Peter Rentfrow, Lewis Goldberg, and Daniel Levitin, was created by breaking down musical genres and building them back up again.

They began by asking thousands of people exactly the wrong question: What were their favorite music genres, subgenres and some examples from each? From that, they identified twenty-six categories. Then they sought out two relatively unheard songs from each category to avoid participants recognizing a song and, say, recalling that it was played at their high school prom. And finally, they played fifteen-second excerpts of the resulting fifty-two songs to another group of people and asked them to rate how much they liked them on a scale of one to nine. Using a series of statistical analyses, they identified five factors that defined each piece of music:

> **Mellow**, *for pop, soft rock, and R&B excerpts perceived as slow, quiet, and not distorted.*
>
> **Unpretentious**, *for country and rock 'n' roll excerpts that tended to be romantic and relaxing.*
>
> **Sophisticated**, *for classical, jazz, and world music excerpts said to be intelligent and complex.*
>
> **Intense**, *for loud, forceful punk or heavy metal excerpts.*
>
> **Contemporary**, *for rap and electronica excerpts—but also jazz.*

Conveniently, these five factors spell out MUSIC. The researchers who developed this model have used it to examine how music corresponds to personality traits, cognitive abilities, and political views.

Some of the same researchers have also tried to extend this broad model from music to all of culture—and it's in this model that we find the beginnings of the Elements of Taste. In their 2011 paper "Listening, Watching, and Reading: The Structure and Correlates of Entertainment Preferences," Peter Rentfrow, Lewis Goldberg, and Ran Zilca came up with what they called a "remarkably clear factor structure" of genre preference "uniquely related to demographics and personality traits." (Unfortunately, this system doesn't have a catchy acronym.)

Their process for coming up with better categories than genres was basically the same: here, instead of using individual songs to build new categories for music, they used individual genre categories across books, television, film, and music to build new categories for all of entertainment. Whereas the MUSIC model dealt with the problems of genre by zooming in—you say you like rock, but do you like "Two Princes" by the Spin Doctors?—the Rentfrow and Goldberg model zooms way out—you say you like rock, but what do you think of nature documentaries? Or murder mysteries? Or sketch comedy?

The researchers began by coming up with a list of 108 genre labels, drawing first from categories on Amazon and similar retailers and then cross-referencing those lists with those generated by three judges. Once they eliminated duplicates, they ended up with twenty-two music genres, thirty-four book and magazine genres, eighteen film genres, and thirty-four television genres. Then they put these lists in front of test groups, some drawn from university students and some from the general public, and asked them to declare their preference for each on a seven-point scale that ranged from dislike strongly to like strongly.

Once they had answers from the 3,227 test subjects, the researchers began looking for ways to group the data. This is where the statistics come in, using complex calculations like scree tests and varimax rotations to sort the data. In simple terms: How many buckets could you divide the responses among before it became impossible to tell which bucket was which?

Here, the math starts to paint a familiar picture. When you split all the preferences into two categories, they look like lowbrow and highbrow. Sitcoms and action movies are in the first bucket, while jazz and *The Economist* are in the second.

When you further divide into three categories, lowbrow splits into what the researchers termed communal and rebellious. Sitcoms are communal, while Bond movies are rebellious. To get to four categories, rebellious splinters into dark and thrilling. Daniel Craig as 007 is dark, whereas Pierce Brosnan is thrilling. And when you push it to five categories, highbrow breaks into aesthetic (jazz) and cerebral (*The Economist*).

Beyond five factors, the sorting system became too specific to be useful. The math suggested either three buckets or five buckets were the cleanest way to sort genres, and the researchers chose five over three simply to ensure they had more detail about who liked what.

Let's pause here and check the contents of our five buckets, like lobstermen pulling up the traps to see what we've caught.

Communal—*Romantic movies, sitcoms, daytime talk shows, pop music, and medical shows*
Dark—*Punk music, horror movies, hip-hop, and erotic films*
Thrilling—*Action movies, science fiction, and cop shows*
Aesthetic—*Classical music, foreign films, poetry, and bluegrass*
Cerebral—*Business books, newscasts, and science shows*

Next, they examined the age, sex, and ethnicities of each bucket, and these conformed to what you'd guess by the genres. To generalize a bit on the sort of person who chooses each category: communal is a less-educated woman; aesthetic is a more-educated woman; dark is a more-educated man; thrilling is a less-educated man; cerebral is an older person, probably a man.

That said, they found that "personality accounted for significant proportions of variance in entertainment preferences over and above demographics."

At this point we should pause to note that this fascinating new road map has brought us to an all-too-familiar place. Many of these findings sound like marketing truisms, especially to those in the culture industries who have a financial stake in knowing these things. You see all those pharmaceutical ads on CNN because old people watch the "cerebral" news. Thrilling action movies are marketed to teenage boys and complex plots take a backseat to fireballs in the third act. The studio audiences of "communal" daytime talk shows are always filled with women for a reason.

There is some truth to these generalizations, and they may well be self-fulfilling. The mere-exposure effect in psychology has shown over and over again that familiarity breeds affinity. Once you're slotted into a category, it's easy enough to make yourself at home.

But you are more than the sum of your age, gender, and annual household income. There is real value in seeing patterns on the map, but we have to explore the territory. When we do, we find a powerful way to think about what we like, and what we might like next. For starters, it becomes easier to see which mash-ups make logical sense (dark and thrilling, for instance, like *The Matrix*) and which are more unlikely (communal and thrilling, like *Star Wars*). Why aren't there more highbrow talk shows, and why does Hollywood have to remake a perfectly appealing foreign film? Check the buckets.

And beyond that, we can take these five categories back to the definitions of taste—and in doing so, we can rethink what we mean when we talk about the difference between taste in food and taste in everything else.

Embodied Cognition, or Why Warm Rooms Are Filled with Warm People

Everyone knows there are two definitions of "taste." What this book presupposes is, maybe there aren't.

The first meaning of "taste" is how our mouths allow our brains to perceive flavor. The second refers to our preferences for just about everything else. What, if anything, do these two definitions have in common? Why don't we just have two words? English, after all, is such a vibrant living language that we are constantly inventing terms like "hangry" to describe ever more nuanced feelings like being irritable while in need of food. Why are we content with letting one five-letter word mean two completely different things?

Because maybe they aren't so different after all. Maybe taste in food and taste in clothes and taste in movies and taste in people are all of a piece. We don't think of them this way, but we act as though this is the case with the words we use. The term for this is "embodied cognition," and it describes the surprising way we think about physical metaphors.

What this means in everyday life is that if you're physically warm, you're more likely to perceive people as friendly, whereas a cold room makes people feel isolated. And the Lady Macbeth effect is real: if you're asked to recall your past transgressions, you're more likely to want to scrub your hands clean.

On a more basic level, neuroscientists have seen that more of your brain is activated when you're told that someone is sweet as opposed to merely nice.

None of the above seem quite . . . serious enough to be true, and indeed there have been issues replicating some of these experiments. But the overall conclusion remains: the mind-body divide is much smaller than we imagine. Of course we *know* that moral cleanliness and physical cleanliness are different, right? On the surface, if we think about it, sure. But deep down, the metaphors we use influence our actions, our opinions and, yes, our tastes. One metaphor for this metaphor is the scaffolded mind: we build on what came before, so simple concepts like sweet candy support more complex concepts, like sweet people. The fact that the words are the same is not a coincidence but rather a sign of a developmental connection between the concepts.

Take sweetness. When you taste sweet foods, you're more likely to behave sweetly toward other people. You'll describe yourself as being more agreeable. And if someone does something nice for you immediately before you eat some candy, that candy will taste sweeter.

Further studies have asked subjects to read either a story of virtue or a story of vice and then drink a bland beverage. The sweeter the story, the sweeter the drink is reported as being—while those subjects in the grip of vice were more likely to call their drinks bitter.

And in their paper "Bitter Taste Causes Hostility," two Austrian researchers presented subjects with bitter tea or water and asked them about their levels of irritation. The bitter tea drinkers were, perhaps predictably, more irritated. Then they offered another group either grapefruit juice or water and asked them what they would do if they found someone kicking the back of their seat in a movie theater. (Their options included: move to another seat, ignore the kicker, become angry but do nothing, turn around and ask them to stop, or turn around and threaten violence.) The grapefruiters were more likely to threaten violence—though less likely to be angry but do nothing (the dictionary definition of "bitter," in the sense of being resentful).

Effects like these hold across much of the world, and similar studies have shown these results in Europe, Latin America, and Asia. There are places where the metaphoric transfer carries different meaning, though. In Israel, for instance, the slang word "*dugri*" celebrates the honest, frank, and forthright culture in which your friend will ask how much you paid for that haircut and then tell you it looks horrible. This cultural premium on bluntness is rare in the world, and it explains why the Hebrew word for sweetness, "*mataktaka*," is less than flattering when applied to people. It means insincere and phony, just as the word "saccharine" does in English. In 2015, a group of psychologists ran similar priming experiments on Jewish men in Tel Aviv, feeding them gummy bears (or not) and then asking them to describe the inauthenticity of a manipulative, successful forty-five-year-old woman with bleached blond hair and Botoxed face. The sweet foods spiked their inauthenticity ratings— while eating spicy foods increased the likelihood that she would be called intelligent.

This outlier aside, we can charge ahead with our taste metaphors, knowing that a connection of sweet people and sweet foods is, for speakers of English and many other languages, a natural link. We can look at how bitter tastes make us feel (spoiler alert: hostile!) and make some further extrapolations about the other basic tastes. And we can link this idea of embodied metaphors to Rentfrow, Goldberg, and Zilca's idea of entertainment dimensions to attempt—wait for it—a Grand Unified Theory of Taste.

The result brings us to the subtitle of this book: "Understanding What We Like and Why." By mapping physical taste onto cultural taste, we can explore a new way of thinking about what we consume. With more insight into our cravings comes the possibility of better satisfying them—or controlling them.

Planning what we eat is second nature, whether you follow a specialized diet or simply make a point of stocking the fridge with your favorite foods. Tools like food pyramids, meal plans, nutrition labels, and cookbooks help guide our consumption.

Planning what we watch, read, and hear is less common, and outside of formal education, there aren't many guides along the way. You're expected to stumble along, using your own wits, resolve, and Spotify's Discover Weekly playlists to figure out what to consume next. This book aims to help with that choice. By categorizing what's out there in a new way, you may consider options you had previously ignored. Or you may find that you were getting bored with the old standbys. Or you might simply find more pleasure in the books, songs, television, art, and film you already love.

Are You Ready to Order?

The four basic food tastes, as any schoolchild can tell you, are sweet, salty, bitter, and sour. Particularly precocious schoolchildren may be able to identify umami as the fifth basic taste, and if they do, they deserve a gold star. To create our Grand Unified Theory of Taste, we can use the idea of embodied cognition to map those five tastes onto the five entertainment factors developed by Peter Rentfrow and his colleagues. That gives us:

Sweet—Communal
Sour—Thrilling
Salty—Dark
Bitter—Aesthetic
Umami—Cerebral

So, does this work? With some slight modifications, yes. The lowbrow categories—communal, thrilling, and dark—map nicely onto the simplest tastes—sweet, sour, and salty. Once your palate becomes more sophisticated, you can appreciate the bitter/aesthetic. And just as the cerebral is a category you need but wouldn't necessarily think of, so too is umami. And then we can map taste to time—tipping our hats toward demography without being beholden to it—as we all start as sweet kids, turn sour in adolescence, become saltier as adults, eventually appreciating the bitter and all the while having an inexplicable draw to the umami.

Note that we are sticking to the five primary tastes, meaning those that correspond to a specific chemical receptor on our taste buds. Spicy foods don't quite fit the bill—you don't taste a habanero pepper so much as you experience the pain of it. (Anyone who has rubbed their eye after chopping habaneros can confirm this.) Furthermore, what we might call culturally spicy falls neatly into the salty category. Recent research has suggested that fattiness might qualify as the sixth basic taste, known as "oleogustus." There may well be a cultural counterpart to fat, something we've been told to avoid for decades but that might actually be good for us, but it's beyond the scope of this book.

Just as on a menu, you are unlikely to find any pure examples of the basic tastes in the buffet of culture. Nearly everything is an amalgam, a blend of two or more of the five tastes to create a unique profile. The categories are only simple on the page; in the real world, everything and everyone contains multitudes. Once you know this and can identify component tastes, you can break down any song, movie, or book. We'll even provide a handy chart to help you do the math. You can figure out what made it taste the way it did, what there was too much of, or perhaps what was missing. And best of all, you can figure out what you'd like to consume at any given moment.

The Elements of Taste can turn the question "What sort of music do you like?" into something more like "Are you ready to order?"

Think of it: When the waiter approaches your table with pad in hand, you know what to do. You understand what spots you want to hit, and you make the best choice with the available information. You scan the menu, looking for an old favorite or an intriguing new option. Any cravings at the moment? Maybe you skipped breakfast and are particularly famished. Maybe you've heard this place has stellar tamales. Maybe you'll follow the lead of your dining companion. Or maybe your eye wandered over to the prices and your inner accountant has advised you to fill up on bread.

The point is you know what you want to eat. And if we take that knowledge and extend it, you'll have an entirely new way of figuring out what you want to see, hear, read, and experience. Are you ready to order?

Palate Cleanser

The Ultimate Taste Test

How can you tell if someone has taste? The logical way would be to inquire after their passions. What are their favorite foods, authors, or cities? It's best to ask these sorts of questions in specific and creative ways to provoke some actual reflection on the matter. What do you always order at your favorite restaurant? What book have you often bought as a gift? Where have you felt most at home?

Jean-Anthelme Brillat-Savarin, the father of gastronomy and a child of the Enlightenment, had an altogether more thorough way of determining the taste of a subject—or rather whether a diner was a human of elevated taste or merely a dull normal. The Frenchman treated the study of the culinary arts as a higher calling, a science that he felt blessed to see come into its own during his lifetime alongside "descriptive geometry and the chemistry of gas." He is credited with the proverb "you are what you eat," though his more elegant phrasing was "tell me what you eat and I will tell you what you are." Gastronomy, he maintained, was "the scientific definition of all that relates to man as a feeding animal," and was what moved "cultivators, vine-dressers, fishermen, huntsmen, and the immense family of cooks, whatever title or qualification they bear, to the preparation of food." It was an equal-opportunity calling, the thing that made food more than mere fuel.

In his exploration of this new science, Brillat-Savarin devised what he called his *"éprouvettes gastronomiques,"* or gastronomic tests. These superlative dishes were scientifically guaranteed to, as one nineteenth-century translator put it, elicit a visible spark of desire or radiance of ecstasy in a well-organized man. The most charming thing about these tests, and a good clue as to why Brillat-Savarin has never been out of print, is that he devised separate *éprouvettes* for different socioeconomic classes. Nearly two hundred years before Pierre Bourdieu, his countryman and fellow occupant of Père Lachaise cemetery, would link taste to class, Brillat-Savarin made it very clear that gastronomes could come from any walk of life. Well, from any of the three for which he devised menus.

As Brillat-Savarin explained, "The power of *éprouvettes* is relative, and must be suited to the habits and capacities of every class of society. All circumstances considered, an *éprouvette* must be calculated to create admiration and surprise. It is a dynamometer, which increases as we approach the higher zones of society."

Brillat-Savarin's societal classes were mediocrity (an income of five thousand francs), comfort (fifteen thousand francs), and wealth (thirty thousand francs or more). Those living in mediocrity would be served veal, chestnut-stuffed turkey, fattened pigeons, eggs à la neige, and sauerkraut with sausage and the finest bacon. The comfortable would enjoy filet of beef, venison with gherkin sauce, boiled turbot, leg of mutton, truffle-stuffed turkey, and green peas. And the wealthy, who would have been wise to skip lunch before this test, would feast upon a seven-pound truffle-stuffed fowl, foie gras, carp, truffled quail on buttered toast, a stuffed pike with prawn sauce, pheasant, one hundred spears of early asparagus, twenty-four ortolans, and a meringue cake.

Assuming you're following along at home and have cooked this for a guest, here is how you know if you've got a gastronome at your table: Upon seeing the spread, the mediocre will announce, "By golly! That looks damned good! Come on! Let's dig in!" The comfortable will say, "What a delightful sight! This truly is a feast!" And the wealthy will chortle, "Sir, what a genius your cook must be! One only eats such dishes at your table!" And in that last statement, your guest will almost certainly be correct.

You may not even need full sentences, though: the author recounts the advice of "a woman of great charm," who noted that you can really tell if a person has taste by listening to their pronunciation of the word "good" as the "real connoisseurs put into this short word an accent of conviction, of pleasure, and of enthusiasm, which people of dull palate can never hope to attain."

Were we to update these *éprouvettes* for both the present day and for our new omnicultural definition of taste, what would they look like? First, we would take Brillat-Savarin's admirable appreciation of the different tiers of society and scale it beyond class to all possible tasters: instead of the host choosing the best thing to serve you, you pick the thing you like the most. It could be a dish, a film, an album, a photo, an exhibition, or an experience. A perfect cheeseburger, a Leonard Cohen song, a Wes Anderson movie, a Rothko painting, or a roller coaster ride. The critical part is that, when this thing is done to your specifications, you are on the record as totally, unabashedly loving it.

Your experience of this perfect thing should match that described by M. F. K. Fisher, translator of Brillat-Savarin and his equal in culinary charm, in her essay "The Pale Yellow Glove": "Once at least in the life of every human, whether he be brute or trembling daffodil, comes a moment of complete gastronomic satisfaction. It is, I am sure, as much a matter of spirit as of body. Everything is right; nothing jars. There is a kind of harmony, with every sensation and emotion melted into one chord of well-being."

Now treat yourself to a particularly fine example of your thing. How much delight does it bring you? Did you exclaim "By golly!" or "What a delightful sight!" or some modern equivalent? Once you've intellectually identified the thing you love, do you emotionally swoon for it? Does your face express your rapture? Do you feel something? That is the modern measure of the gourmand: you know what you love, and then you show what you love.

2

Sweet: The Taste of Innocence

Featuring: GLUCOSE, CUTENESS, HELLO KITTY,
SITCOMS, *MURDER, SHE WROTE,* BEANIE BABIES,
"CARELESS WHISPER," AND, ABOVE ALL ELSE, KINDNESS

> *They surfeited with honey and began*
> *To loathe the taste of sweetness, whereof a little*
> *More than a little is by much too much.*
>
> —SHAKESPEARE, *KING HENRY IV*, PART I

There's a good argument to be made for taking candy from a baby: babies shouldn't be eating candy. But try explaining that to the bawling infant. She was enjoying that lollipop before you wrenched it out of her sticky hands, and now her mother is giving you a look. The fact is that sugar is the taste of safety. We evolved to know that if something tasted sweet, we could probably eat it without dying (or at least, not dying immediately). Sweet is the one taste we all like

Sweet is the one taste we all like from birth.

from birth. The brain needs glucose, and it points the tongue in that direction. Our ancestors who lacked this tongue-brain wiring didn't get around to reproduction.

When you equate sugar and safety, the obesity epidemic has a new underlying theme: these truly are comfort foods. And like the spoiled kid with a menagerie of stuffed animals piled on his bed, we've unconsciously decided that if a bit of sugar identifies food that's safe to eat, few scoops more signal food that's even better. So we add sugar to bread, spaghetti sauce, and sliced cheese, turning every meal into dessert. The irony is that the high doses of sugar we ingest as part of the Western diet are likely toxic in their own right, meaning this flight to more and more safety is putting us in peril. Too much of a good thing can be wonderful, as Mae West said, which in this context makes it entirely appropriate that there's a Quebecois variation on the Twinkie named for the burlesque star.

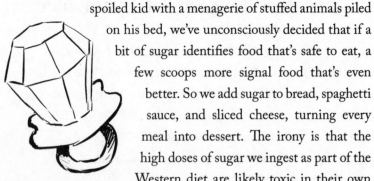

But there are signs that our appetite for sugar knows some bounds. Soft-drink sales in the United States have been dropping since the late 1990s, with the amount of full-sugar soda consumed by the average adult dropping 25 percent—despite the fact that no fewer than forty flavors of Mountain Dew were introduced in that time. To not even slow your shopping cart's roll as you pass the Mountain Dew Game Fuel Electrifying Cherry display? Well, that suggests a real change in the American consumer's tastes. Still, this is a gradual rollback, and sweetness shows no signs of giving up its spot as the most popular of the five tastes.

Sweetness as safety carries over into the broader culture. There is always an audience for safe works of art—the plays, movies, and shows that end with a wedding, a sunset, or at the very least a group hug. Children's entertainment is understandably cuddly, but it's quite possible to continue consuming age-appropriate sweetness throughout your lifetime. Sitcoms that reinforce the nuclear family, animated films made with gentle pop-culture references for parents and big-eyed characters for the kids, coloring books for adults. Even murder mysteries—books centered around the violent taking of another human's life, the least safe event imaginable—have a subgenre called the cozy.

To use another word, sweetness is cute. In 2001, *The Onion* published an article with the headline "Area Woman Judges Everything By Whether It's Cute." The subject of the satirical article "uses the word 'cute' more than 150 times a day, applying it to everything from such traditionally cute items as infants and stuffed animals to such nontraditional items as board games, soft-drink bottles, and art."

In 2014, "while working on a research paper exploring female consumers' brand-driven retail decision making," three marketing researchers felt compelled to point out that the word "cute" kept recurring in their interviews. At first it passed unnoticed because the researchers were male and "tended to use the word when referring to a baby, or a puppy." The women they interviewed, however, "used the word to describe products, brands, people, stores, and even regarded it as a state of being."

As usual, there was more than a grain of truth in *The Onion*'s story, and it was more than a grain of cultural sugar. The female's traditional role as primary caregiver is the classic evolutionary explanation for why women are primed to appreciate cuteness.

Sweet culture is uncomplicated, accessible to all, lighthearted, gentle, and—for all these reasons—popular. It's often what we get when we don't make a choice. It's sometimes where we go when we're confronted with difficult circumstances. It's usually at the heart of otherwise inexplicable fads. And it should never be written off as dumb. Too much sweetness is unavoidable in modern life, but too little—or none at all—makes life barely worth living. Group hug!

Kawaii: The Sweet Society

There is no nation on Earth more saturated in cultural sugar than Japan. There, sweet culture is the universally beloved *kawaii* style.

According to the scholar Sharon Kinsella, by the early 1990s "*kawaii*" was "the most widely used, widely loved, habitual word in modern living Japanese." And what, exactly, does the word mean? "Aside from pastel colors, a compositional roundness, the size of the eyes, a large head and the short distance from nose to forehead, quite often it is things or people that are not trying to be cute," writes Manami Okazaki in her 2013 book on the phenomenon. So it's a sort of authentic cuteness, the attribute babies and kittens come by naturally and that makes Hello Kitty worth a billion dollars a year.

Some scholars trace *kawaii* back to 1914, when the illustrator Yumeji Takehisa opened a Tokyo shop geared exclusively to school-girls. Marketing to this demographic was virtually unheard of, which makes his first customer the patient zero of our era's obsession with youth culture. He sold illustrated books, prints, and dolls that featured cute patterns of things like mushrooms and umbrellas, and he described the aesthetic he was aiming for as "*kawaii*."

The *kawaii* culture began in earnest in the early 1970s as a very specific handwriting style embraced mainly by teenage girls using mechanical pencils. The English penmanship equivalent would be dotting your *i*'s with hearts, but this was exponentially more stylized—rounded letters, kittens frolicking between words, hearts and the English word "love" randomly inserted into text. This underground fad—think of them as the ancestors of emojis—wasn't particularly legible and was banned in some schools, which of course had the effect of making it more popular.

Around the same time, slang that sounded like baby talk began to spread, and with it a penchant for acting like children. Hello Kitty and scores of similar round and large-eyed characters were introduced and plastered on everything from rice cookers to credit cards.

Sweet foods were a key part of *kawaii* culture, and as in English, the word for sweet can refer to both food and people. In Japan, ice cream was a growth industry throughout the 1980s, despite the population's high genetic likelihood of lactose intolerance.

So why *kawaii*? Kinsella posits that the cold industrial economy needed to soften its edges. "Cuteness loaned personality and a subjective presence to otherwise meaningless—and often literally useless—consumer goods and in this way made them much more attractive to potential buyers," she writes. That economic need twinned nicely with the country's culture of respect for inanimate objects, a deference central to the Shinto faith and perhaps best seen in the annual Festival of Broken Needles, during which seamstresses ceremoniously insert their used sewing needles into a block of tofu. (Or more popularly in *The Life-Changing Magic of Tidying Up*, in which Marie Kondo encourages her disciples to thank their dirty socks after a hard day of being trod upon.)

And then there's the fact of Japan's aging population. In 2014, the Land of the Rising Sun had the distinction of being the world's fastest-aging nation, with more than a quarter of its population over the age of sixty-five. It's reminiscent of the P. D. James dystopian novel *Children of Men*, in which a global fertility crisis ends childbirth and humans treat their pets as children. With a relative lack of real small people, there's some logic in adults acting like kids and making mundane consumer products look like toys.

More pointedly, the artist Takashi Murakami has argued that *kawaii* is indicative of "the tragic apocalyptic paradise that is Japan today," a cultural reaction to Japan's childlike relationship to the United States since the end of World War II. He made specific reference to this in the 2005 exhibition he curated at the Japan Society in New York, cleverly titled "Little Boy: The Arts of Japan's Exploding Subculture." In addition to referencing the name of the atomic bomb dropped on Hiroshima, Murakami points out that his country's artists depicted the most horrible weapon ever created as a dinosaur. Superflat is the name he gives to all of this 2-D culture, in the sense that all of the country's complex fears and anxieties are flattened into cartoons.

In the extremes of *kawaii*, these anxieties come into raised relief. *Kimo kawa* is one form of this, "*kimo*" being an abbreviation of the word "creepy" and "*kawa*" a short form of "*kawaii*."

The Chinese artist Lu Yang hit both of these marks with "Kimo

Kawa Cancer Baby," which exhibited in Shanghai in 2014 and consisted of brightly colored sculptures of googly-eyed tumors chewing on human organs, animations of Cancer Babies, and a looping, upbeat song with the refrain "We are happy cancer cells." The artist's intention, she told the *Lancet*, was to negotiate the irony of the natural world. "Some people hate it because they hate cancer, and they think I'm using disease and death to make fun, but some people think we should face the reality and not avoid it."

The artwork, given *kawaii*'s emergence as a response to grim realities, is less an ironic twist than a natural extension. The unnatural extension is *guro kawaii*, or the grotesque cute. Gloomy Bear, a life-sized homicidal pink bear generally depicted spattered with blood, is perhaps the best example of *guro kawaii*. Introduced in the year 2000 by the Osaka artist Mori Chack, the origin story of Gloomy has him adopted as a cub who, as he is an actual bear, eventually attacks his human owner. Chack has said the idea came after he saw a news report about a bear attack and decided to inject "a sense of that terror in that cuteness."

Though this strand of *kawaii* culture is often depicted as shocking—"This isn't *kawaii*. It's disturbing."—is a typical blog reaction—in the case of Gloomy Bear, it's really just taking the *kawaii* aesthetic and applying it to reality.

"Some may think, 'Drawing pictures of bears attacking children is cruel,'" Chack writes on his website. "Has anyone noticed that, in my work, I have embedded my opinion that humans are the most brutal creatures on earth?" The observation is an extension of Murakami's theory. In these mutations of *kawaii*, we see sweetness blended with sour thrills, salty darkness, and bitter art. And we see how a balanced and sophisticated cultural diet can be built on a sticky-sweet base. *Kawaii* starts from innocence but encompasses all aspects of life.

In Japan, every town and city has at least one *yuru-kyara*, a word that loosely translates as "mascot" but has more than a trace of animism about it. They are all varying degrees of *kawaii*, and in a very real way, these creatures are the places they represent. When an earthquake struck the city of Kumamoto in April of 2016, killing tens and injuring hundreds, there was a social-media outpouring of concern for Kumamon, the region's rosy-cheeked bear *yuru-kyara*. The mascot's eventual reappearance, as Neil Steinberg describes it, was pure catharsis.

"Three weeks after the April 14 earthquake, Kumamon visited the convention hall of the hard-hit town of Mashiki, where residents were still sleeping in their cars for protection as 1,200 tremors continued to rumble across the area. The visit was reported on TV and in the papers as news, as if a long-sought survivor had stumbled out of the wreckage alive. The children, many of whom had lost their homes in the earthquake, flocked around him, squealing, hugging, taking pictures. Their friend had returned."

TASTING NOTE: COLDPLAY

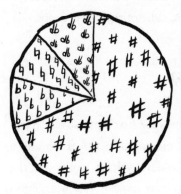 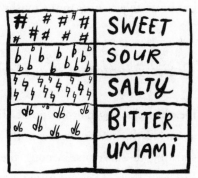

Sweet: 70 percent
Sour: 10 percent
Salty: 10 percent
Bitter: 10 percent
Umami: 0 percent

When the world first heard Coldplay announce they were all yellow in the year 2000, the British band sounded a lot like mid-1990s Radiohead. By that point Radiohead was off exploring new sonic dimensions, leaving Coldplay to double down on ballads. Soon the emotional piano pop of Chris Martin and his bandmates was everywhere, and in the parlance of those times, you were either with Coldplay or against them. Their music is sentimental but stadium-sized, a less-specific U2, designed to make you cry without knowing why. They have sold millions of albums, yet hating Coldplay is as prevalent a pop-cultural opinion as you can get. Why? Because we expect a rock band to be thrillingly sour or defiantly salty, with the occasional bitter concept album. Coldplay hits those notes when necessary—a political statement here, a song with Rihanna there— but invariably returns to the mushy middle of their sweet spot.

Cozies: Murder without Death

Death is the original plot point. The very first stories were likely about death, functioning as both a memorial to the fallen and a warning to survivors. Among the oldest written works are the Pyramid Texts of ancient Egypt, which are basically a reincarnation manual for recently deceased pharaohs. (The fact that pharaohs had to be dead to read them also meant this was the first paywall in re- corded history.) Tragedies were the first of the Greek genres, Shake- speare's greatest plays are his tragedies, and there's a reason you should never bet on a comedy to win best picture.

Another common thread that goes back to the beginning of narrative: pattern recognition. We learn from others' mistakes and get a small thrill when we can use previously assimilated knowledge to figure out where a story's going to go. It's life as a giant crossword puzzle.

Combining these two phenomena explains the enduring appeal of the murder mystery, and the serial format. Once you figure out whodunit, it's on to the next Maigret mystery, or Miss Marple story, or Hercule Poirot adventure, or Sherlock Holmes case. The more of them you read, the more you want to read, and even if you get better at figuring out which of the hired help was responsible (hint: the butler), getting to the end still scratches a deep itch.

But what if there were a way to enjoy the thrill of solving the puzzle without having to think about death, however fictionalized? Could you, in other words, reformulate the murder mystery to play down the murder and play up the mystery?

This is, in essence, the sub-genre known as the cozy. The most well-known example is not a book but the long-running TV series *Murder, She Wrote*, on which mystery author Jessica Fletcher solved homicide after homicide in the small Maine town of Cabot Cove. In print as on television, these are what we might call gentle murders. Writing about the then-new literary trend in 1992, *New York Times* crime columnist Marilyn Stasio declared these books "remarkable for their nonthreatening content and non-violent characters." She identified the characteristics of a cozy, which include amateur and usually female detectives, small-town settings where "the atmosphere is designed to give pleasure and comfort," and as little violence as is possible.

Erin Martin, the self-proclaimed "cozy mystery list lady" and proprietor of cozy-mystery.com, describes the genre as follows:

> *Most often, the crime takes place "off stage" and death is usually very quick. Prolonged torture is not a staple in cozy mysteries! The victim is usually a character who had terrible vices or who treated others very badly. Dare I say . . . the victim "deserved to die"?*

Once the unpleasant business of the homicide is dealt with, tea can be made and puzzles can be untangled.

The cozy genre covers a wide swath of territory, some parts of which are self-consciously silly and others that are no less gripping for their lack of grit.

Louise Penny's series featuring Chief Inspector Armand Gamache, head of homicide for the Sûreté du Québec, are harder cozies, and she has eloquently explained why her particular take on the murder mystery wasn't about the murder.

"That's simply a catalyst to look at human nature," she told *Publishers Weekly* in 2009. "They aren't about blood but about the marrow, about what happens deep inside, in places we didn't even know existed."

Or as Charles Isherwood put it in a *New York Times* review, "Ms. Penny's books mix some classic elements of the police procedural with a deep-delving psychology, as well as a sorrowful sense of the precarious nature of human goodness, and the persistence of its opposite. . . ."

And then there are the cozies that feature knitting patterns (*Knit One, Kill Two, Needled to Death,* and *Purl Up and Die*), cats (some of whom can talk and others who don't; the two camps have their fierce devotees), or recipes (Diane Mott Davidson's bestselling series featuring caterer Goldy Shulz, who perfects recipes and solves crimes in titles like *The Whole Enchilada* and *Dying for Chocolate*).

The audience for these books is, not surprisingly, older and female. A US survey conducted in 2010 found 70 percent of one thousand mystery readers polled were female and over the age of forty-five. The older readers were less interested in darker stories, and 40 percent of the respondents said they were always in the middle of a mystery.

When we look at where mysteries fall in the entertainment categories, there's a pretty even split between communal and thrilling. A mystery TV show is slightly more thrilling than communal, while a mystery novel is thrilling, communal, and aesthetic, in that order. If we wanted to amplify the communal aspects, we'd play up the focus on people and relationships.

In our system, that means we'd ensure the overall taste was more sweet than sour. And for a mystery in particular, that means playing up the characters and the puzzle, playing down the thrills and adventure, and making sure the story as a whole was not so challenging as to slow consumption. It needs to be a solvable puzzle, in other words.

And that's the recipe for a genre so durable it's an industry. The cozy trend rises and falls. It began in earnest as a gentle backlash to Thomas Harris's *The Silence of the Lambs*, when it became apparent that a significant portion of the marketplace would prefer Hannibal Lecter's meal of a human liver with fava beans and a nice chianti to be a bit more . . . cruelty-free. The cozies were challenged again by Stieg Larsson's *The Girl with the Dragon Tattoo* and all the dark Nordic noir that followed. And the genre suffered some self-inflicted wounds from, in the words of Marilyn Stasio, authors "who seem to think that all you have to do is make the hero an idealized version of yourself, fabricate some anecdotal situations for an eccentric group of characters attending a cooking school, solve a murder or two over dessert, incorporate a few recipes into the text and put a cat on the cover."

There are always serial killers lying in wait, and sometimes they steal all the attention. But like a cat finding his way to his owner's lap, the cozies always come back: challenging, comforting, and just sweet enough to leave readers wanting more.

Bronies: Finding Sweet Solace

When I was a child, I spoke as a child, I understood as a child, I thought as a child; but when I became a man, I put away childish things.

—1 Corinthians 13:11

When I became a man I put away childish things, including the fear of childishness and the desire to be very grown up.

—C. S. Lewis

What happens when society expects you to grow out of your taste for the sickly sweet, but the sweet tooth persists? You may find yourself the only adult in a roomful of children. You may find it difficult to share your enthusiasms with your peer group. You may find yourself the target of some concerned glances. You may be a brony.

The bronies were incepted on October 10, 2010, when a reboot of the *My Little Pony* animated series titled *My Little Pony: Friendship Is Magic* debuted on The Hub, a little-watched American cable channel. Like pretty much every other animated series from the 1980s, the original *My Little Pony* was just a show-length advertisement for toys based on the characters—so really, the characters were based on the toys. This was the case with He-Man, Transformers, Strawberry Shortcake, G.I. Joe, and many more. What marketers today call native advertising—creating ads that are indistinguishable from the actual content the ads theoretically pay for—was standard programming fare for a generation of children. And Hasbro, the corporate rancher who owned those ponies, was also a part owner of The Hub.

To bring *My Little Pony* back to the small screen, the company turned to Lauren Faust, a writer and artist on *The Powerpuff Girls*. Faust helped redesign the characters in a distinctly anime way: larger eyes, brighter colors, sparklier sparkles. To look at a My Little Pony from the 1980s next to one from the 2010s is like looking at a dinosaur next to a bird: evolution in action. Similarly, the plots and pacing were radically updated to fit into a significantly smarter popular culture. Since the rise of Pixar, it had become expected that animated films have at least some appeal to the adult chaperones of the target audience, and the ponies were no exception. Faust was the perfect person to make this happen: as a fan of the original *My Little Pony*, she felt a duty to bring some intelligence to the magical land of Equestria. "If we give little girls a respectful interpretation of the things they like—if we dare to take it as seriously as they do—we will see for ourselves that it's not so silly after all," she wrote in a foreword to *The Elements of Harmony*, the snappily named official guidebook to the series. "We can truly appreciate the merit they see in it. And, amazingly, we can enjoy it for ourselves."

That "we" included people like Luke Allen, a thirty-two-year-old computer programmer who told *WIRED* magazine in 2011 that the "weird alchemy that Lauren Faust tapped into when she set out to make the show accessible to kids and their parents hooks into the male geek's reptilian hindbrain and removes a lifetime's behavioral indoctrination against pink." Hence bros who like ponies, or bronies.

The hive mind of that particular reptilian hindbrain was 4chan, an anonymous bulletin board site that, as both supporters and detractors would agree, represents the purest state of what a particular corner of the Internet can be. According to a history of the brony conversation written by Una LaMarche in the *New York Observer*, it was actually an opinion piece on a comics news blog decrying the corporate control and lack of creator control in the new *My Little Pony* that first raised interest in the reboot. "Nobody denies that The Hub's shows will perform well and fulfill the programming needs of the network," wrote Amid Amidi on Cartoon Brew. "But then again, nobody suggested that *Smurfs*, *Snorks*, and *Pound Puppies* wouldn't do well in the 1980s either."

"It was pretty alarmist, but it also got a lot of us going over to watch the show," original brony Nanashi Tanaka told LaMarche. "We were going to make fun of it, but instead everybody got hooked. And then the first pony threads exploded."

And so the 4chan community was the first to ask what everyone who encounters a brony must eventually think: Is this for real? And if so, is there something unsavory about it? This conversation took a much more obscene form, of course, which only reinforced the brony message of love, friendship, and rainbows. An awkward truce was reached, but not before the bronies spread onto the wider web.

As the name Hasbro began to describe the company in a new way—they now *had bros*, whether they wanted them or not—the merchandisers made sure these grown men had plenty of collectibles to collect.

"We are sort of stepping back and seeing how the customer is interacting with our brands in a way we haven't dreamed of and we like to see where it is going," the company's senior vice president of franchising and marketing told the trade magazine *License! Global*, though the article made clear that "[t]he Hasbro evergreen is typically marketed to young girls ages three to six, and Hasbro admits the series' growing adult fan base is a surprise." Cultural studies journals called it transgressive fandom; business analysts called it a lucrative market.

So to reiterate: Is it for real? And if so, why do grown men like culture designed for little girls? The answer to the first question is undeniably yes, and the proof is both how long the subculture has been around and how much its members have spent on merchandise. (At a basic economic level, if you like something ironically and buy mass quantities of it, your irony has become a moot point. Ask anyone who wears Old Spice deodorant.)

So why do bronies exist? It's been argued that it's because *My Little Pony: Friendship Is Magic* caters to them with inside jokes, like an homage to *The Big Lebowski* (Jeff Letrotski is introduced in season two when the ponies go to a bowling alley) or an elaborate *Star Wars* montage. This is true, though these elements were only introduced in the second season, another sign of Hasbro's marketing savvy. Back when the first season caught on, critics suggested that the simple cartoon plots were appealing to young men specifically because they *didn't* try to be clever and knowing. So maybe these two sides of the same argument effectively cancel each other out. A similarly suspect rationale for the bronies is the high-quality animation of the show—but if that's all it takes to get men into cartoons, why didn't *Frozen* become *Brozen*?

One of the more convincing theories was floated by Mary H.K. Choi in *WIRED*, and it goes like this: The 1980s versions of these commercials-as-cartoons were horrible, but the toys they sold were cool. Kids had epic playdates with the ponies, and they remember those moments fondly. "Armed with the toys, we churned out urfanfic that spackled over the holes left by the shows' crappy dialog and lazy mythology," Choi writes. So the new shows, which are better in every way, remind viewers of their childhood playtime.

Why didn't Frozen *become* Brozen?

Except heteronormative men who grew up in traditional 1980s households likely never played with My Little Ponies. (Hasbro sold them G.I. Joes.) So how are they nostalgic for something they never had? The Portuguese word "*saudade*" may fit the bill. Deeply linked to the Portuguese and Brazilian temperaments, it was described by the Englishman A.F.G. Bell as "a vague and constant desire for something that does not and probably cannot exist, for something other than the present, a turning towards the past or towards the future, not an active discontent or poignant sadness but an indolent dreaming wistfulness."

And isn't any BronyCon, as their conventions are known, a gathering of indolent, wistful dreamers?

Yet more brony research—and there is an impressive amount of it—conflicts with this theory, as, in the words of one cultural studies researcher, "many Bronies claim to be unfamiliar with previous *My*

Little Pony incarnations and some even show disdain for the earlier versions, which suggests that nostalgia is not much of a factor in their dedication to *FIM* [*Friendship Is Magic*]."

This academic, Venetia Robertson, discusses all of the above possible explanations for bronydom—the animation style, the in-jokes, the pop-culture references—before ultimately settling on a simpler but deeper motivation: a need to belong. "The ponies provide an avenue for authentic self-expression and reification within the bosom of a community that supports and shares these goals. Bronies are not just among fellow fans, men, and geeks, but individuals turning to anthropomorphic animal media to seek an authentic experience of selfhood." In this sense, *My Little Pony* is an oddball example of cultural preference at its most basic: members of the same tribe like the same things, and liking those things admits you into that tribe.

In other words, everypony needs to be somepony, somewhere.

The best way to understand the bronies is, of course, to see where they fall in the Elements of Taste. From this perspective, their fandom makes perfect sense. Sweetness is all about that which is lighthearted, gentle, and focused on relationships, and it skews young and female. It would be hard to identify a cultural artifact as purely sweet as *My Little Pony: Friendship Is Magic*.

The first-wave bronies (yes, that's what we're calling them) emerged from the depths of Internet culture, an arena that is alternately more sour, salty, bitter, and umami than it is sweet. Sweetness, then, is what they were missing. And by using *My Little Pony* to fight back against their 4chan antagonists, they unwittingly created a movement—one that was eagerly encouraged by a multinational toy company. The lesson here is that you never lose your sweet tooth, and though age and gender may change how much of it you require, you still need some sugar; it's called a universal taste for a reason. The central premise of *My Little Pony: Friendship Is Magic* is that each pony represents one element of harmony and only by working together (friendship!) can they ultimately triumph (magic!). By embracing their sweet sides, the bronies are finding balance.

They're also finding that there's more to life than *My Little Pony*. As Shaun Scotellaro, the founder of brony hub Equestria Daily, reflected wistfully on the ebbing popularity of his passion in 2015: "There is no denying that 2012–2013 was our major fandom peak," he wrote. "This was that point in time where it was essentially 'the thing' to rock a Rainbow Dash avatar on your favorite message board or gaming service."

But though his brothers had moved on, he insisted their love survived, nurtured with plastic merchandise and at conventions. His bronies could run free, "and the massive core base that is always here welcomes them back with open hooves." Take it as good news for everyone except maybe Hasbro: bronyism, defined as an unexpected and unrestrained love for all that is sweet, will live on long after Pinkie Pie, Twilight Sparkle, and the rest of Equestria have been put out to pasture.

TASTING NOTE: *FRIENDS*

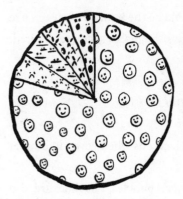 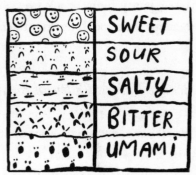

Sweet: 80 percent
Sour: 5 percent
Salty: 5 percent
Bitter: 5 percent
Umami: 5 percent

Sitcoms are sweet by definition: Lighthearted, communal, over in twenty-two minutes, and full of hugs. The audience should laugh with the characters, relate to their problems, and (in the days before binge-watching) look forward to seeing them at the same time next week. In other words, these attractive, tightly scripted, two-dimensional people should be our friends. Ergo, *Friends*. The six well-off, straight, white, twentysomething New Yorkers were like family to one another—and to thirty million viewers on Thursday nights from 1994 to 2004—without actually being family. There had always been sitcoms focused on friendships instead of family or work relationships, but none so sweetly as *Friends*. Whereas *Seinfeld* prided itself on "no hugging, no learning" and *Cheers* followed a bunch of middle-aged barflies, *Friends* was a sitcom about warm, young, pretty, funny people who would be there for you 'cause you're there for them too. It remains the most huggable sitcom ever aired.

Beanie Babies: Cultural Sugar Highs

We all like sweet things—but what happens when we *all* like sweet things?

There are housing bubbles and tech bubbles, but there are also a significant number of bubbles that smell like bubblegum. In these collective sugar highs, the communal side of sweetness can look a lot like a stampeding mob.

The history of bubbles traditionally begins in Holland in the 1630s, when the Dutch came down with a bad case of tulipomania. Bulbs of the flower commanded ludicrous prices, and every Dutchman, Dutchwoman, and Dutchchild jumped into the market. As Charles Mackay's famous (if not entirely accurate) book *Extraordinary Popular Delusions and the Madness of Crowds* put it: "In 1634, the rage among the Dutch to possess [tulips] was so great that the ordinary industry of the country was neglected, and the population, even to its lowest dregs, embarked in the tulip trade."

Why tulips? Not because they had any practical use, but precisely because they didn't. Holland was the wealthiest nation in Europe at the time, and with that wealth came a desire for some conspicuous consumption.

The beauty of the tulip bubble is that it was based on beauty; if people thought that this particular commodity would forever increase in value, it was in part because they simply liked the way it looked.

And in that respect, Beanie Babies were the tulips of the United States in the 1990s.

How exactly Beanie Babies grew into a phenomenon that eclipsed such previous toy hits as Cabbage Patch Kids is a lurid story told in Zac Bissonnette's 2015 book *The Great Beanie Baby Bubble*. The elements included "localized variations in knowledge about rare Beanie Babies," the emergence of the Internet as a cultural force, and a vigorous legal strategy. There were stories of average people making huge amounts of money from stuffed bears. (This fed what economists call the greater fool theory: any price can be justified if you think someone will pay more.) And then came eBay, a perfect place to auction Beanie Babies for whatever the market would pay.

But most of all, it was because they were cute. Creator Ty Warner knew how to make a sweet plush toy—in a word: eyes. They need to be well-spaced, shiny, and never, ever obscured by fur. And Warner invested enough in the process—even trademarking the word "poseable"—to set his products apart on toy-store shelves. As one reseller told Bissonnette, the Beanie Babies were "something really cute that just brought out the worst in people." They were collected by "creepy, belligerent men" and couldn't be given to kids with cancer because their parents kept trying to confiscate and resell them. Then there was the sad tale of a murder that resulted from a fight over Beanie Babies, leading to the defining quotation of the Beanie bubble: "I cannot go to prison as the Beanie Baby Killer. I'm gonna have to kill someone else just to get my credibility back."

Even after the crash, the sugar high had a lasting effect. Just as tulipomania created Dutch horticulture, the Beanie Baby boom helped create the Internet as an economic force. Is it too much to say we are living in a world built by Beanie Babies? Yes, it is. But still.

Our natural affinity for pretty, useless things doesn't always have to end in ruin. Sometimes, under the right conditions, we can sustain ourselves for generations on a steady drip of sweetness. Consider the prettiest commodity of them all, the soft, shiny metal hoarded throughout history because of its—well, why *is* gold so valuable? You may well ask yourself that when you're gnawing on your hoarded ingots after the apocalypse. For now, though, just be happy you didn't stockpile useless flowers or poseable stuffed animals.

Sweet Sounds

"I've never seen you looking so lovely as you did tonight," Chris de Burgh crooned. "I've never seen you shine so bright."

That was the most I could take. I was sitting in an airless office, volunteering my time to stuff envelopes for a reputable charity. The radio was locked on the local lite-rock station, which may or may not have featured *E* and *Z* in its call letters. Its smooth tunes at a reasonable volume helped the middle-aged staff ease through their workday, but my late-adolescent eardrums would have preferred a sharpened pencil. In between ads for mattresses and weight-loss clinics, they played the most excruciating music. Phil Collins, Elton John, George Michael, and Billy Joel were the four horsemen of my mind-numbing afternoon, and they were at the service of Mr. de Burgh. I wanted this volunteer-service line on my résumé, but at what cost?

The day I heard "Lady in Red" twice in an hour—my second time volunteering—I submitted my resignation. Well, not really: I just told the nice lady with the jar of Werther's Originals on her desk that my coursework was too demanding to allow my further stuffing of well-intentioned envelopes. I didn't tell her this music was torture. I didn't tell her that if young men in their teens and twenties had been invited to the Geneva Convention, easy rock would have been inserted right between drowning and electrocution. Also, there would have been a lot more horseplay.

For the decade or so that followed, I managed to keep a safe distance from any sort of lite, light, EZ, easy, smooth, diet, or soft rock. I would opt for indie, math, sweater, hard, or, in a pinch, Kraut rock, but never anything easy. Sure, there was some Belle and Sebastian in there, but those sensitive Scots wouldn't dare turn on a synthesizer unless it was really, really necessary.

In that sense, I was unthinkingly going through the taste-making process that Carl Wilson elegantly described in his 2007 masterpiece *Let's Talk About Love: Why Other People Have Such Bad Taste*. Wilson has a much better—or much worse—Chris de Burgh in Celine Dion, and he works through his disdain so thoroughly in the book that by the end, listening to "My Heart Will Go On" nearly brings him to tears. Nearly: "While my eyes didn't well over, neither were they completely dry."

My evolution was much less profound, as it was spurred by a

conversation with a friend about perhaps the most benign subject two young men can discuss: the late and lamented Guitar Hero. He had spent a weekend playing it, and I confessed that I hadn't gotten the hang of the video game.

"I just don't have any rhythm," I told him.

"Is it because you have guilty feet?" he asked.

"Ha," I responded. "My feet were never formally charged."

From that, the earworm had been planted. Those tawdry saxophones were ringing in my ears. I found myself looking for the Phil Collins song "Guilty Feet" the next day at work, only to learn that it was *George Michael* who had named his song "Careless Whisper."

Once I'd watched it on YouTube a few times, I was hooked. I heard it while waiting in line at IKEA and found myself swaying to the beat, arms full of tea lights. I promptly made it my karaoke song.

Everybody wants to rule the world.

From Mr. Michael, the slide into back-to-back commercial-free soft-rock hits was a steep one, and I had company on the descent. Because everybody knows these songs. Everyone wants to know what love is. Everybody wants to dance with somebody. Everybody wants to rule the world. And then there's "Africa," a song that first irritated me on K-Tel commercials but now speaks to me on a deep, danceable level.

How did this happen? I didn't think through my tastes and prejudices. It just happened. Occam's razor would suggest that I had simply become lame. The fact that I thought *Tron: Legacy* was way too loud would seem to back that up. But for the sake of my self-esteem, let us discount that possibility.

The same researchers who developed the MUSIC model discussed at the beginning of this book later examined how musical preferences change throughout our lives, and they confirmed some cultural truisms: young people listen to more music in more contexts than people in middle age, and with age comes less interest in the intense and contemporary and more time for the sophisticated. "Raising a family and pursuing a career provide adults with defining features of their identities. It seems reasonable to suggest that the meaning derived from these roles diminishes the function that music serves in shaping identity and offering fulfillment," the researchers write. It doesn't have to define you; it just has to fill the background.

There is some comfort in knowing I'm not alone. The cultural reappropriation of easy listening is happening, albeit in a niche way. Take "As Above So Below," a Klaxons song remixed by Justice that's actually a distorted cover of the Doobie Brothers' "What a Fool Believes." The original was a song my father would play on repeat on family road trips, and it was rendered suitable for a sweaty dance club. Bands like Miami Horror and Chromeo back this up with their reinterpretations of Supertramp and Hall & Oates, respectively. But while they may offer some artistic cover for my cravings, they can't really satisfy them like the originals. They're like drinking a Jones Cola with real cane sugar when all you really want is that high-fructose corn syrup Coke fix: unarguably better but not what hooked you in the first place.

If rock 'n' roll is all about rebellion, frustration, and youth—the sour—then lite rock is about conforming, adapting, and aging. It's sweet, but just a bit bitter. In "Lady in Red," he's not trying to pick up that gorgeous babe; he's just appreciating her again for the first time. "Someone Saved My Life Tonight" expresses relief over avoiding a loveless marriage. These songs are not designed to be cranked while taking Dad's car to the mall. They're for when Dad's car is your car. They're all kind of sad, actually: that melancholy nostalgia that once again calls to mind the bittersweet phenomenon of *saudade*.

(In this respect, the origin story of "Careless Whisper" only improves the song. George Michael wrote this singular work of art when he was seventeen. He had never been in a serious relationship. All of the lyrics are bits of melodrama he picked up while working as a cinema usher. It's a gloss on a gloss, a Hollywood version of doomed romance perfected by a clever kid and embraced by actual adults the world over. Who better to mope over lost love than a precocious teenager?)

And maybe that's why I finally began to appreciate lite rock. It's been documented that the glummest time of life is early adulthood. Stress, worry, anger, and sadness all creep toward their lifetime peaks in middle age. But once you get past your midforties, you're statistically due to start feeling better about things. At that point, I may be ready to turn up the Public Enemy. Until then, well, it's a little bit funny, this feeling inside. Deep inside, I hope you feel it too.

TASTING NOTE: *THE NOTEBOOK*

Sweet: 100 percent
Sour: 0 percent
Salty: 0 percent
Bitter: 0 percent
Umami: 0 percent

The 2004 movie that launched the careers of Ryan Gosling and Rachel McAdams is the cultural equivalent of high-fructose corn syrup. The whole setup is that the aged pair (played by James Garner and Gena Rowlands) are reminiscing about their temporarily unrequited love as recorded in (yes) the Notebook, removing any doubt that they end up together. To call it formulaic is an understatement; this is a movie that found new resonance in Hollywood's oldest story through flawless execution. Boy meets girl, boy loses girl, boy wins girl back, boy kisses girl in the rain, boy and girl live long, fulfilling lives together and die in each other's arms.

Throw in World War II, James Marsden, and a Ferris wheel, and you've got a Hollywood romance sweet enough to rot the teeth of an entire generation.

Sweet Smarts

The knock against sweetness, both in physical and cultural taste, is that it is so frequently overdone. Just as there is sugar added to spaghetti sauce for no good reason, so too are happy endings added to movies whether they make sense or not. In both instances, the result is cloying.

Our world is so saturated in sugar that it's only logical to limit your intake after a while. But while a sugar-free diet may actually be nutritionally sound, cutting out sweet culture is as inadvisable as it is difficult.

Sweetness is correlated with innocence, and is inversely proportional to experience. The common extension of this is that warm and fuzzy feelings are for children, and the older and more educated we become, the harder our hearts must get. There's the old saw about how if you're not a liberal when you're young, you don't have a heart, and if you're not a conservative when you're old, you don't have a brain. The underlying logic is that as the heart's power recedes, the brain must take over.

In fact, the opposite is true. The writer George Saunders explained this simple concept in his speech to the 2013 graduating class of Syracuse University. As a recipient of MacArthur and Guggenheim grants, Saunders is as certifiable a genius as exists in literature. The one piece of wisdom he chose to impart, above all others, was to simply be kind to one another.

By his reasoning, this shouldn't be something you know as an innocent child and forget as an experienced adult, but rather the opposite. As you age and if you are lucky, you will realize there are three fundamental lies we all start out believing:

"(1) we're central to the universe (that is, our personal story is the main and most interesting story, the *only* story, really); (2) we're separate from the universe (there's US and then, out there, all that other junk—dogs and swing-sets, and the State of Nebraska and low-hanging clouds and, you know, other people); and (3) we're permanent (death is real, o.k., sure—for you, but not for me)."

The older you get, the fewer excuses you have for not questioning these beliefs. As Saunders points out, everything from friendships to religion to education to children serves to teach us that it's not about us. We are small, temporary, and insignificant— with the ability to become kind, loving, and luminous, should we choose this route. This idea is represented throughout culture by the Kindhearted Simpleton, or the Moral Moron. He is Shakespeare's Falstaff and Dostoyevsky's Idiot, Hanks's Forrest Gump, and Buscemi's Donny Kerabatsos.

This may be so hard to grasp because it's so simple. Missing this point is confusing the sweet with the saccharine.

Sweetness, then, is the starting point but also the ideal place to end up. It's the middle part—the experience that comes after innocence but before awareness—that we're prone to get stuck in. If sweet culture is defined by people and relationships, it really is the thing that matters. All the other tastes are worth sampling, to be sure, and there are great things to be found in their many combinations and permutations. Ideally, though, you come back to a note of sweetness. And then you really appreciate it.

"Because kindness, it turns out, is *hard*," Saunders told the graduates. "It starts out all rainbows and puppy dogs, and expands to include . . . well, *everything*."

Palate Cleanser

A Brief and Painless History of Taste

Taste was invented in 1963, right before the first Beatles LP. Before that, people wore, watched, ate, and listened to whatever was at hand. This explains the popularity of vaudeville, radio dramas, and boiled cabbage.

Though the above is undoubtedly accurate, it is still worth zipping through a highly subjective chronology of the many inadequate ways people have tried to categorize what they are consuming.

So let us introduce Thorstein Veblen, who foresaw the use of Instagram in 1899 when he coined the term "conspicuous consumption." The industrial revolution created a leisure class, and that leisure class announced its existence by buying things everyone else would notice. Those things had to be better than everyone else's things, which required taste. At the same time, the aristocracy had to let the world know that, ahem, they got to the money first. To do so, they needed things that were even better than those of the leisure class, meaning they needed even better taste. And there you had the high-, middle-, and lowbrow.

In a 1949 *Harper's* cover story, Russell Lynes famously defined what high-, low-, and middlebrow meant to the modern United States. "It isn't wealth or family that makes prestige these days," he wrote. "It's taste and high thinking."

The article went from highbrow to middlebrow when *Life* magazine summarized it and included a fantastic chart delineating exactly what was Low Brow, Lower-Middle Brow, Upper-Middle Brow, and Upper Brow in a range of categories. For instance, from low to high in drinks were beer; bourbon and ginger ale; "a very dry martini with ginger ale"; and finally "a glass of 'adequate little' red wine."

This essay and chart, compiled at the time of the GI Bill and the Book of the Month club, is imbued with the idea that America's newly affluent and educated middle class is taking over, whether the highbrows like it or not. "They live everywhere," Lynes writes. "They are the members of the book clubs who read difficult books along with racy and innocuous ones . . . They are the course-takers who swell the enrolments of adult education classes . . . They eat in tea-shoppes and hold barbecues in their backyards . . . They are hell-bent on improving their minds as well as their fortunes."

From here, taste moved from cultural criticism to social science. The ultimate arbiter of taste in the twentieth century was a Frenchman with a penchant for page-long sentences. Pierre Bourdieu packed his 1979 book *Distinction: A Social Critique of the Judgement of Taste* with abstractions, complications, and terminology, all of which combined to make him the preeminent sociologist of his time. Using research he conducted in 1960s France, Bourdieu drew on Marxist thought to devise a theory in which taste's primary purpose is to maintain the class system. It is cultural capital, and it was distributed along the same lines as economic capital: the richer you were, the more taste you had. Or more specifically, your taste could most likely be predicted by how much education you had and what your father did for a living.

Bourdieu illustrates this with a survey showing that the educated upper classes (those whose "conditioning by negative economic necessities," or wealth, "tends to induce an active distance from necessity") will say that a cabbage, a butcher's stall, or a scrap yard would make a good subject for a photograph, whereas the less cultured would choose more obviously beautiful subjects like a folk dance, a sunset over the sea, or a first communion. Taste was socioeconomic identity.

Bourdieu's theory revolutionized sociology, but in practice it was somewhat leaky. For instance, the aforementioned cabbage that only the wealthy could see as worthy of a still life? As Roger Friedland wrote of Bourdieu's own research in 2009:

> To imagine it beautiful, you've got to hold coleslaw, the low price of cabbage, and flatulence at bay. But in the case of cabbage, only 7 percent of the working class, 11 percent of the middle class and 18 percent of the upper classes think it would make a beautiful

photograph. Most French people don't think it can be pretty. . . .
[A]bout half of each of the three classes—working, middle,
upper—think it would make a meaningless photo. As for most
other cultural practices French social classes are not culturally
distinct.

And it seems that the further you get from 1960s France, the less the theories hold true. For instance, in 1990s Australia, sociologists found a wide variety of interests and activities that didn't correspond with any socioeconomic group:

Watching the football on Saturday, playing beach cricket,
growing giant pumpkins for the show, driving a stock car,
walking a bush trail, doing voluntary work for a service club,
playing bridge, gardening, working out, going to the movies or
to a dance club . . . each of these is diversely configured and spe-
cifically valued in ways that do not sustain generalization.

Thus came a sociological update of Bourdieu's ideas: what used to be snobs and slobs has become omnivores and univores. The omnivore, in this day and age, is the person with a taste for reflection—it's not about knowing exactly which dead German composer you like the best, but having some knowledge of Brahms and garage rock and K-pop and ska and whatever else demands your attention. The univore is the person who likes very specific genres. So by extension, the wider the variety of culture you appreciate and consume, the higher class you are. (One study even came up with a metric for that gap, a way to quantify the distance between the lowest- and highest-status music you like. The highest grade of omnivore, according to that study, is someone who likes both New Age music and rap.)

This in turn has been picked apart by Bourdieu's disciples, who argue that while it may appear that today's upper classes like a wider variety of culture, they crack under intense questioning and revert to the old snobs versus slobs.

And then there's the distinct possibility that both theories could apply in real life, to snobs, omnivores, and even omnivore snobs. And the so-called short-range omnivore may consume a large quantity of culture but specifically avoid the "legitimate" culture of opera and classical music, thus confounding the sociologists. The most damning critique of how confused all this talk of -brows and -vores has become may well be this passage from a 2014 paper in *Poetics*:

> *The highest grade of omnivore, according to that study, is someone who likes both New Age music and rap.*

"At issue in these debates are the reality of this shift, the importance of its impact, its nature, its substance, and so forth. However, while reading these articles, one is sometimes left with a sense of confusion: What exactly are they talking about?"

It's a good question: What *are* they talking about? It seems that much of the confusion in modern studies of taste goes back to where we began: how the studies are done. As we saw, asking people what genres they like is a surefire way to stumble into the Bassey conundrum ("Some people won't dance/If they don't know who's singing/Why ask your head?/It's your hips that are swinging").

Pierre Bourdieu could ask his head and get an answer. When

your primary lens on culture is classical music, it's possible to sort and classify. But Pierre Bourdieu didn't anticipate Taylor Swift. Modern genres may overwhelm the head, but the hips still swing. And as Shakira reminds us, hips don't lie. So to figure out what we like, we need a new way to determine what there is to like. And that's how we arrived at the Elements of Taste.

3

Sour: The Taste of Rebellion

Featuring: WARHEADS, CRUSHED SMURFS, SYLVESTER
STALLONE, THE BRIX/ACID RATIO AND JOHNNY ROTTEN.

Too much sugar is bad for your smile. After the third slice of
cake, you may be excused. And in the traditional development
of our palates, when we're ready to move on from sweet, we choose
sour.

This phenomenon was famously observed by Charles Darwin,
who wrote in 1887 that his own children "strongly preferred the
most sour and tart fruits, as for instance unripe gooseberries and
Holz apples." Research done more than a century later found that a
third of children between the ages of five and nine had a strong
preference for sour tastes, and that "their preferences increased with
increasing levels of citric acid."

These sour patch kids explain why mouth-puckeringly acidic
candies are a huge business, despite the fact they taste horrible to
much of the population. It wasn't always this way. Licorice, boiled
sweets, mints, chocolates, and gumdrops filled the candy counters
of yore. It wasn't until the 1970s that Pop Rocks and Martians (later

rebranded as Sour Patch Kids to capitalize on the Cabbage Patch Kids craze of the early 1980s) came to be. By the late 1990s, if it wasn't extreme—or, preferably, Xtreme!!!—it wasn't worth putting on the shelf.

"A Tootsie Pop's chewy center was good enough for coonskin-capped *Davy Crockett* fans in the '50s, but modern youngsters demand candy that spins, luminesces, or plays music in their heads," Mark Frauenfelder wrote in *WIRED* in 1999.

The same article introduces a man who is the perfect bridge between sweet and sour: Peter De Yager. After making his fortune by bringing sweet gummy bears to the United States in the 1980s, De Yager reproduced his formula in the 1990s with a sour candy. He told *WIRED* about some of the supersour Japanese candies he tried in the early 1990s. One, called Super Lemon, "was so sour that most people would take it out of their mouth immediately, throw it in the wastebasket, and almost be angry at you. You thought you'd have an enemy for life."

Unless, of course, those people were in the sweet spot of sour appreciation, and De Yager knew such a target market existed. He also knew they'd love a supersour confection he'd discovered in Taiwan, and that they'd appreciate a cartoon of a man with a mushroom cloud erupting from his skull, to be named Wally Warhead, and thus Warheads were born. They were a fad, a craze, a lasting brand, and a $40 million business De Yager sold to another company in 2004.

What made them so successful? The answer to that question will also point to the appeal of sour in general, both as a physical taste and as a cultural one.

One theory is that children who like sour foods are looking for, in the words of one paper, "adventures, thrills and excesses." Research has suggested that children who enjoy sour candy are more willing to try new foods and are drawn to the brightest-colored package. And once they discover they love something that the majority of the world can't stand, well, there's your membership card in a secret society. Some candy manufacturers have pushed that button hard, inciting low-grade moral panic around sour candy. Around the time of Warheads' ascendancy, a tart powder called Crave was banned in cities and towns across the United States because authority figures feared kids only liked it because it looked like cocaine. With flavors like Cloud Nine and Psycho and packaging that resembled a plastic vial, it was specifically designed to upset adults.

"It's sort of the Pixy Stik of the millennium," a Crave spokeswoman told the *Hartford Courant* in 1997, and she added that "we're a very edgy company." The white variety of Crave was taken off shelves because of complaints, but the neon flavors continued to be sold.

A seventh grader interviewed for the story said that "it tastes good and it looks cool," and even alleges that he has seen students selling Crave to each other for up to $1.25 a vial, nearly twice the retail value. Crave was sour by taste and sour by culture: thrilling, rebellious, and undeniably adolescent.

Sour culture—the thrilling genres that included action, adventure, science fiction, and Westerns—is a mildly transgressive way to choose something just far enough from being sweet that it's a different taste—but not nearly as unfamiliar as salty, bitter, or umami culture. You know, for kids.

So why do adults like sour candy? There's no need for scientists to study this question, as two of "the biggest candy fans on the Internet" examined the question in a 2016 episode of their podcast Candyology 101.

"I use sour or spicy candies a lot when I need to stay energized or stay focused," said Cybele May, editor and writer of candyblog .net. "I like a sour candy when I'm driving long distances because it keeps my mouth wet (so I don't have to drink a lot and so I don't have to stop a lot) and it keeps me focused on driving."

Her colleague Maria Smith more closely approximates the child's presumed point of view: "by having something sour, I think it kind of wakes you back up, so you can appreciate things more."

Sour culture is all about waking you up. In that respect, it's the most one-dimensional taste. It is nothing more than a thrill. Once you're awake—once you've been thrilled—you probably want something more substantial. Pairing sour with sweet, salty, bitter, or umami is a surefire way to make sure you're paying attention to what comes next. But just sour is, well, just sour. This is why it's very rare to find a purely sour cultural experience; an entire movie of BASE jumping would have a limited audience, and probably only on IMAX.

Sour culture is a starter, but it isn't sustainable. Look deep into the bulging eyes of Wally Warhead. They're just black dots in circles. The mascot's head is a mushroom cloud. He is sour, full stop, and as the package warns, "eating multiple pieces within a short time period may cause a temporary irritation to sensitive tongues and mouths." Sour is best in small doses.

Sloche: Adolescence on Ice

If you want to guess the tastes of a teenage boy, it's often useful to think of what a normal, well-adjusted adult would like—and then imagine its opposite. No marketer has had more success with this strategy than Couche-Tard, a Quebec-based chain of convenience stores whose name literally translates as the teen-friendly "goes to bed late." In the late 1990s, the company decided it could be doing more with frozen drinks. Their research showed that 72 percent of twelve-to-eighteen-year-olds had purchased slush the previous year, and that slush was this target market's sixth-most-purchased item, after gum, candy, chocolate, soft drinks, and chips. Remember this was in Quebec, where winter lows of zero degrees Fahrenheit (–17 C) are not uncommon.

The leader in this category was the Slush Puppie, a noncarbonated iced slush drink sold around the world. (There are no 7-Elevens in Quebec, so the Slurpee didn't register.)

Their research also revealed that teenagers are, well, teenagers. From that they devised the brand mission: "To satisfy their need for sensory gratification and protest against authority, parents and society." The Slush Puppie mascot, a docile white hound in a toque, clearly had no such ambition. The resulting ads were designed to repel adults, and they worked.

The early varieties of Sloche, Couche-Tard's proprietary slush drink, were Full Zinzin, Bomme Galoune, Sang Froid, Schroumph Ecrase, and Goudron Sauvage, which should be appreciated in their Quebecois beauty before we translate them: Totally Crazy, Gubble Bum, Cold Blood, Crushed Smurf, and Wild Tar. The blue Sloche's name was soon changed to Winchire Wacheur, complete with the option to drink them out of windshield washer fluid containers. It's unclear whether this was because the owners of the Smurf brand objected or because that particular variety wasn't selling, but the idea that Couche-Tard would pick a fight with a beloved toymaker clearly fit the brand mission.

Sloche was a huge hit right from the start, outselling Slush Puppies by a factor of four to one. Based on mainstream media mentions, adults hardly noticed the branding at first. With every year, a more disgusting variety would be unveiled, and a 25 percent boost in sales would follow. Pureed Chick, Rosebeef, and Wonton Soup all managed to be both gross and high-grossing.

In 2006, they introduced the Liposuction variety, described in the *Montreal Gazette* as follows: "The pale rose shade is, I suppose, intended to conjure up cellulite and other fatty matter aspirated out of a human body during liposuction surgery. A dispensing machine presided over by a blobby mascot churns the drink into a plastic cup with a bubble top and a jumbo straw for sucking it back."

When the Sloche turned ten, their ads featured clowns being shredded into confetti, prompting complaints from the clown community. "Why do they use my profession? Why don't they use a policeman and see how they feel?" said Giovanni Iuliani, a retired clown formerly known as Patapouf. In the resulting Canadian Press story, a perfectly on-message Couche-Tard spokeswoman responded that "We're trying to reach teenagers, people between the ages of thirteen and eighteen. They really like our campaigns, so I don't care if older people don't like them."

What is not part of the Sloche story in any appreciable way is the flavor of the drinks. Just as they have nothing to do with the marketing, they have nothing to do with the names chosen or even the color of the product. The Rosebeef flavor, marketed with pictures of a Sloche cup filled with rare roast beef held aloft by a crazed butcher, was so named because it was pink. It tasted like peach. Similarly, the Tropical Cheddar color was orange, but the flavor was sour apple. Perhaps the strangest was Paparmane, which referenced the chalky peppermint candies favored by senior citizens, was pink, and tasted like grape.

Sloche shows how cultural taste can have almost nothing to do with actual taste, even if the preference in question is a food product. No one really cares what the the drink tastes like, as long as it's cold and syrupy. The taste is sweet, but the overall impression is sour. They use the cultural sour to get you in the door, and everything after that is sweet.

The impressive run of the Sloche may have ended in 2016. The Pizzaghetti flavor, which mixed red strawberry and yellow kiwi flavors and references a Quebec mash-up dish that features the two Italian classics, appears to have been the final installment in the annual campaign. A new advertising agency has placed a hashtag in front of the word Sloche and debuted a series of unremarkable ads that show teens holding longboards, playing with smartphones, taking sips of their drinks, and experiencing a digital-art interpretation of a brain freeze.

"After fifteen years of successful campaigns, this was a difficult decision to take," the agency vice president said. "We had to part with the idea of always doing new flavors. But I believe it was time to put the product, and the Sloche name, at the heart of the message." That message, spoken in French but also in the universal language of corporate-speak, now seems quite comfortable with authority, parents, and society. Pure sour never lasts.

TASTING NOTE: *MAD* MAGAZINE

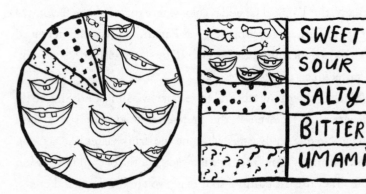

Sweet: 5 percent
Sour: 80 percent
Salty: 10 percent
Bitter: 0 percent
Umami: 5 percent

From the mid-1950s to the mid-1990s, *MAD* magazine was the official periodical of adolescent sourness. Everything from politics to culture was fodder for The Usual Gang of Idiots, and the result was a comprehensive questioning of all authority. In the words of legendary editor William Gaines, "Editorially, we're trying to teach them, 'Don't believe in ads. Don't believe in government. Watch yourself—*everybody* is trying to screw you!'" As such, the magazine didn't run ads, a distinction it shared with only *Consumer Reports*. Despite the age of its readership, it lampooned movies they couldn't or wouldn't see ("Hennah and her Sickos") alongside more obvious targets ("The Empire Strikes Out"). From personal experience, I can attest that LBJ's Great Society, the Vietnam War, Watergate, and Iran-Contra could all be reasonably understood by a close reader of *MAD*'s back issues. After Gaines's death in 1992, *MAD* slowly became a more traditional and less interesting magazine, accepting advertisements and paying closer attention to its target demographic. Once again, sour fades away.

The Last Action Hero

The summer blockbuster was born on June 20, 1975, when *Jaws* premiered, but it took almost another decade before all the brains had been bred out of the genre, leaving only brawn. The pure action movie was a creature of the 1980s. Anything with Dolph Lundgren, Jean-Claude Van Damme, or auto-pilot Schwarzenegger qualifies: The leading men had to have a certain steroidal swagger, and that was it. Acting skill or facility with English were so optional as to be expendable—and indeed, Sylvester Stallone has helpfully collected every one of these action heroes (plus Frasier, for some reason) for his *Expendables* exercise in beefcake nostalgia.

These movies were very definitely of a time and place. In 1982, *First Blood* introduced John Rambo as a Vietnam veteran with posttraumatic stress disorder. It followed in the bootprints of a series of post-Vietnam films and was gripping if pulpy, with Stallone still shining from his Academy Awards for *Rocky*. The sequels, in 1985 and 1988, turned the conflicted soldier into a one-man army. The bitter notes were gone, leaving only the sour. *Rambo: First Blood Part II* was panned by critics and loved by audiences, grossing more than three times the box office of the first film. In *Rambo III*, Roger Ebert estimated that Stallone spoke all of two hundred words in the entire movie. Shoot first, talk later—or preferably not at all.

The formulaic nature of these films was practically chemistry. Though the grammar doesn't quite make sense, the website Seagalology outlines the Steven Seagal recipe down to the title: "Two or three words (usually) going by: 'verb preposition noun' or 'verb article noun.' For instance, *Out for Justice*, *Above the Law*. There can also be two prepositions or a preposition and an article or conjunction if needed, i.e., *Out for a Kill*. Two-word titles should go by the formula: 'verb noun' or 'adjective noun.' . . . Extra points if you can stick the words 'Steven Seagal Is . . .'" right before the title and have it make sense."

A purely sour taste is only so interesting, and these films eventually began to add more elements. John Woo stylized the genre with balletic violence, slow-motion sequences, and thick clouds of white doves. In *Pulp Fiction*, Quentin Tarantino deployed genre thrills in a way mainstream cinema had never seen before. Both mixed some bitter with the sour and ended up with a far more palatable product.

Now, in the era of J. J. Abrams and Joss Whedon, it's a given that every action movie will have a modicum of intelligence, wit, and self-awareness.

Even Jason Statham, as pure an I-do-my-own-stunts action

hero as you could ask for, mocks himself. As his character bragged in Paul Feig's movie *Spy*, he makes "a habit out of doing things that people say I can't do: Walk through fire, waterski blindfolded, take up piano at a late age."

There was a time and place for the purely sour action movie, but these days that sort of movie (pauses, leaps out of exploding freight train, looks at camera, brushes dust off shoulder, winks) has become expendable.

TASTING NOTE: INDIANA JONES

Sweet: 40 percent
Sour: 50 percent
Salty: 0 percent
Bitter: 5 percent
Umami: 5 percent

When George Lucas dreamed up Indiana Smith (as the archeologist was originally named), the filmmaker was directly channeling the adventure serials of his youth. "Saturday matinee serial—that was the initial thought," he told *Vanity Fair.* To bring it into the 1980s, the magazine's Jim Windolf wrote, these adventures needed a "little more care, better production values, and a dash of irony." (Irony, for our purposes, is composed of equal parts bitter and umami.) The result was a franchise that defined 1980s cinema, the perfect mix of sweet and sour, thrills with jokes. The elaborate gross-out banquet in *Temple of Doom* was supremely sour and thus perfectly aimed at preteen audiences. Sadly, the resulting wave of interest in archaeology as a career path crashed into the dusty wall of reality: there's little use for a bullwhip in a real excavation.

Sweet and Sour: Marvel's Magic Formula

As we've identified sour as the natural taste progression from sweet, it makes sense that they'd work so well together. The balance of the two is appealing enough to have a dipping sauce named for it, and with good reason. In the world of food science, this is known as the Brix/acid ratio, where one degree Brix is the equivalent of one gram of sucrose dissolved in one hundred grams of solution. When this ratio is perfected, people can't stop eating the product. This is often the case in perfectly ripe fruit, so you could say that nature had this golden mean figured out long before Adolf Brix came up with the measure of sweetness that bears his name.

The Brix-to-acid ratio is often the best way to tell if a fruit has reached maximum deliciousness. To quote one finding, "Brix/acid ratio was found to be the best objective measurement that reflected the consumer acceptability and can be used as a reliable tool to determine the optimum harvesting stage of Crimson Seedless table grapes."

So how do table grapes compare with television shows? According to Peter Rentfrow's research, the entertainments that max out both communal and thrilling are real-life mysteries, police and legal procedurals, variety shows, and animated films. Ideally, these programs balance a focus on people and relationships with a few thrills. A good ensemble cop show has this mix as well: the detectives bust the bad guys and then chum around back at the precinct. If they get wacky enough, you can get into action-comedy territory, a mash-up that often doesn't work (*Stop! Or My Mom Will Shoot*) but occasionally shines (*Spy, Hot Fuzz*).

Any action film that focuses on a team hits the mark as well. Look, they're all working together to destroy Ultron or whoever, and the only way they can be beaten is if they're turned against each other. This is the Marvel multiverse formula, one that has churned out huge box-office earnings from comic-book characters with very little name recognition. You may not know who Hawkeye is, but he's friends with the Hulk, so he must be good people.

Finally, the sweet-sour combo hits that perfect age of preteen adventure. It's thrills without danger, just enough excitement to raise your heart rate but not enough to worry you. The tang of sour against the backdrop of sweetness is a very particular taste, but as Adolf Brix described and Marvel Studios demonstrated, once you perfect it, people won't be able to stop consuming it.

TASTING NOTE: BLARPING

Sweet: 0 percent
Sour: 60 percent
Salty: 10 percent
Bitter: 10 percent
Umami: 20 percent

To understand BLARPing, you need to start with LARPing. "LARP" stands for live-action role-play, and it's the sort of thing generally associated with Civil War reenactments and Dungeons & Dragons. The *B* in "BLARP" stands for "business," a subgenre devoted to emulating prosaic office culture. One of the pivotal figures in the history of BLARP is Thomas Oscar, an Australian teenager who started a Facebook group for a fictional company called Stackswell & Co. in 2013. As he told *Fast Company*, "an office just seemed like the easiest thing to role play, take the piss out of senseless bureaucracy." A bunch of punk kids sending each other pretend e-mails about synergy and jammed photocopiers was so cleverly subversive as to be self-defeating: eventually real-life office workers started to join the group. Instead of teens smirking at the soulless hellscape of cubicle culture, it became cubicle dwellers guffawing about how funny it would be if their coworkers were iguanas. At which point the sourness ended and the teens left.

Sour and Salty: The Taste of Punk

Who among us hasn't, at one time or another, wanted to be sedated? And in that desire, we see the eternal appeal of punk rock.

What made the Sex Pistols so amazing? the rock critic Greil Marcus asked in *Lipstick Traces: A Secret History of the Twentieth Century.* His answer came in book form, but to sum it up, it was their embodiment of the deeply suppressed desire to kick over the coffee table of polite society, possibly set it on fire, and perhaps proceed to urinate upon it. It is sourness in its most rebellious form, and Marcus sees it as a hidden thread through the 1900s, linking the Dadaists, sound poetry, the Lettrists, the Situationists, and other anarchists in highly improbable ways.

It's fitting, then, that in this most defiant art form we have to defy the researchers who inspired this system. They found that punk rock was almost entirely dark, ranking above even horror films or heavy metal. In our version, that makes it salty: intense, edgy, and hedonistic. And while all those elements are certainly there, it's no coincidence that teenagers are the most susceptible listeners to the atonal yawp of Mr. Rotten.

Johnny Rotten's aim, Greil Marcus writes, was "to take all the rage, intelligence, and strength in his being and then fling them at the world; to make the world doubt its most cherished and unexamined beliefs; to make the world pay for its crimes in the coin of nightmare, and then to end the world—symbolically, if no other way was open."

The band's biggest hit was timed to be its most notorious moment: "God Save the Queen" was released right before Elizabeth's Silver Jubilee in 1977. Linking Her Royal Highness to a fascist regime and singing that she wasn't a human being hit all the soft spots: Factories refused to print the album, radio stations refused to play it, stores refused to sell it, and the charts refused to list it. The Kingdom was United against the Sex Pistols, and in spite (or because) of that, the song was enormously popular.

"God Save the Queen" ends with the words "no future, no future, no future," and if you look at the time and place in which it was released, it's quite clear what fans had to feel nihilistic about. Britain of the 1970s was a country of rolling strikes, lost empire,

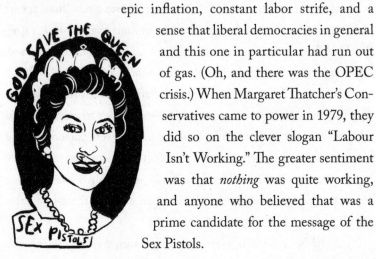

epic inflation, constant labor strife, and a sense that liberal democracies in general and this one in particular had run out of gas. (Oh, and there was the OPEC crisis.) When Margaret Thatcher's Conservatives came to power in 1979, they did so on the clever slogan "Labour Isn't Working." The greater sentiment was that *nothing* was quite working, and anyone who believed that was a prime candidate for the message of the Sex Pistols.

Contrast that with the Silver Jubilee celebrations. If everything was falling apart, why was everyone putting on a happy face to celebrate the twenty-fifth anniversary of the queen's accession to the throne? Such a commemoration was the epitome of sweetness: people coming together to engage in pleasant, lighthearted celebration. It was perfectly countered with something sour: a rude, rebellious, and adolescent finger in the eye of anyone who cared to gawk. It turned salty from there—hedonistic, dark, aggressive—but the initial shock was the thrill of seeing Her Royal Highness's face with a safety pin through the royal lips.

Teenage rebellion is generally rooted in the realization that adult society is full of lies and propaganda, that it doesn't make any sense. The world of the 1970s was one in which nothing seemed to work, where all governments seemed out of ideas. In the West, they called it malaise; in the Soviet Union, they invaded Afghanistan. To call the whole thing a fraud wasn't exactly illogical.

And boredom: it's hard to underestimate the importance of boredom in adolescence. How much creation, destruction, and rock music has been birthed simply because there was nothing else for teenagers to do?

When the punk moment of the late 1970s passed, the aesthetic lived on as the uniform of teenage rebellion. Leather jackets, skinny jeans, Doc Martens, piercings—even clean-cut rebel Ferris Bueller fashioned his hair into a Mohawk. The howling rejection of the modern world is rarely part of the look. The punks were salty back in the days of the Sex Pistols, but time has washed most of that away. What's left is a distinctly sour aftertaste.

Palate Cleanser

The Wisdom and Foolishness of Crowds

If you were to look out your window one day and see a mob assembled on your front lawn, you would understandably be concerned. Mobs, by definition, are out to cause trouble. They often carry torches and pitchforks. They do not generally respond to reason. *The Simpsons* makes a point of including an angry mob in just about every season, and as Principal Skinner memorably said while brandishing a sledgehammer in the episode "Bart After Dark," "There's no justice like angry mob justice!" The mob is dumber than the sum of its parts.

But as Francis Galton famously demonstrated in 1906, the mob—or more accurately, the well-behaved attendees at the West of England Fat Stock and Poultry Exhibition—could also be spookily smart. He asked eight hundred people to guess what the weight of an ox would be after it was "slaughtered and dressed."

"The judgments were unbiased by passion and uninfluenced by oratory and the like," Galton wrote in *Nature* the next year. "The sixpenny fee deterred practical joking, and the hope of a prize and the joy of competition prompted each competitor to do his best. The competitors included butchers and farmers, some of whom were highly expert in judging the weight of cattle; others were probably guided by such information as they might pick up, and their own fancies."

All in all, Galton estimated, the average voter probably knew as much about ox weights as he (and it was definitely a he) knew about political platforms. With low expectations, the cards were counted, and when the exact middle vote of 1198 pounds was chosen—the vox populi, as Galton called it—it was correct to within one percentage point of the actual weight of 1207 pounds.

"The result is, I think, more credible to the trustworthiness of a democratic judgment than might have been expected," Galton concluded.

The experiment has been repeated many times since, with similar results. The NPR show *Planet Money* did it with a picture of a cow posted on their website in 2015, and the average of the seventeen thousand guesses came to within 5 percent of the cow's actual weight.

All of which is amazing, but it doesn't explain angry mobs or Internet comment boards. Crowds can, in certain instances, be wise. They can also all start wearing harem pants for no obvious reason. What makes them pick wisdom over dropped crotches?

> *What makes them pick wisdom over dropped crotches?*

Jaron Lanier addresses this in his 2010 manifesto *You Are Not a Gadget*. The reason the crowd can guess the ox's weight, he explains, is that "there's at least a little bit of correctness in the logic and assumptions underlying many of the guesses, so they center around the right answer." It's not that this magical crowd thinks for itself; it's that the individual thinkers in the crowd are more often right than wrong, and an ideal filter was put in place to isolate this rightness. Calling them thinkers also puts a fine point on it: When individuals in a crowd think, they're wise. When they don't, they're mad. So how do you get them to think?

Lanier takes some steps toward a "wide-ranging, clear set of rules explaining when the wisdom of crowds is likely to produce meaningful results." The crowd shouldn't frame its own questions, should answer by secret ballot, and—most important in the realm of taste—should only address questions with simple answers like a number. In other words, the question format should hew as closely as possible to that of the Fat Stock and Poultry Exhibition.

The real world is rarely like that. There is the pressure of conformity, to not be the weirdo in the gray suit when everyone else is wearing a blue suit. You may well prefer a blue suit primarily because you won't have to think about suits while you're wearing it. But more insidious is the idea of social proof, the assumption that if everyone's waiting in line at the new ramen place, it must be good. The more people follow this logic, the less logical it becomes. Which is why we need to think for ourselves, and what the Elements of Taste are all about.

4

Salty: The Taste of Experience

Featuring: NAUGHTY POSTCARDS, CHRISTOPHER NOLAN,
DISCO RIOTS, NIGELLA LAWSON,
AND CHOCOLATE-COVERED POTATO CHIPS

If we start off sweet and then turn sour, when do we get salty? The answer is contained in the first pages of Mark Kurlansky's *Salt: A World History*.

There, Kurlansky introduces Alfred Ernest Jones, a Welsh psychologist, the official biographer of Sigmund Freud, and the author of a 1912 essay that claimed mankind's fascination with salt was just a stand-in for sex. And while it is true that people once believed mice became pregnant after eating salt, it's also true that sometimes a saltshaker is just a saltshaker.

That said, the word "salty" can mean racy or risqué, with sexual overtones. It can also mean crude or coarse. Or old and experienced. Or, as it's most popularly used now, upset or angry. Or more specifically, how you mockingly describe someone who's upset or angry. It's with this definition that "salty" was voted 2014's word Most

Likely to Succeed at the twenty-fifth Word of the Year proceedings of the American Dialect Society. This usage was traced back to black American vernacular in the mid-twentieth century, particularly as used in the phrase "jump salty." (A particularly jaunty 1935 example from the *Philadelphia Tribune*, as sourced by Ben Zimmer: "Now as far as France and Italy were concerned, Hitler was jumping salty, spreading that jive.")

In recent years, it began appearing in online discussions of fight video games—in particular, the Salty Suite describes a hotel room where two gamers will meet for a one-on-one grudge match.

And if we're being literal, "salty" can also describe the presence of the sodium ion, a chemical that is crucial for maintaining the body's water balance. It's an element that's best in small doses but that nearly all Western cultures vastly overconsume.

All of which doesn't actually answer the question: If sweetness describes childish tastes and sourness correlates to adolescent defiance, where does saltiness fit in?

In our list of entertainment preferences, it maps onto genres "characterized by intensity, edginess, and hedonism." And so we can say it is later adolescence and early adulthood: a time of independence, sexual awakening, and self-awareness.

Coarse, ribald, naughty, angry: These are the salty tastes of experience. Compare and contrast with the sweet tastes of innocence. These songs of innocence and songs of experience are well paired, as William Blake and Bono both know. By comparison, the sour songs of rebellion are on the B side. So while salty and sour share a certain piquancy, there's something much more complex about salty tastes. There's just more flavor there, and we crave them on a deeper level.

Salty culture is absolutely necessary but best in small doses. In that respect there's a strong argument to be made that, just as we eat too much sodium, we consume too much cultural salt. You don't have to be a churchgoing moralist to notice the sex, profanity, and nihilism that saturate our entertainment. When it's used properly, salt is well-placed profanity in a play or an anchovy on your pizza. It's just vulgar enough to make you enjoy what's around it. Too much and you become the shipwrecked sailor, surrounded by water and dying of thirst.

Please pass the salt.

Salty Postcards and George Orwell

If you want to find something salty, go to the seashore. That's where, for most of the twentieth century, Britons could admire the artwork of Donald McGill. His paintings, and those of his many imitators, adorned thousands of postcards and earned him the title (as per the *Daily Mail*) "forefather of the cheeky postcard industry." And it was indeed an industry. When picture postcards were officially sanctioned by the Royal Mail in 1894, it didn't take long for pictures of landscapes and lighthouses to give way to something with a bit more tang. Often, that took the form of what one historian describes as "cheap gags featuring caricatured holidaymakers in generally embarrassing encounters, often lavatorial or ripe with sexual innuendo."

The archetypal McGill postcard features a tweedy young man

and a demure woman in a clingy dress sitting under a tree. The caption reads:

"Do you like Kipling?"

"I don't know, you naughty boy. I've never kippled!"

The stereotypes that filled these cards were described to the literary set by George Orwell in a 1941 essay for the magazine *Horizon*.

"Your first impression is of overpowering vulgarity," Orwell writes, after spreading a dozen McGill postcards on a table. "This is quite apart from the ever-present obscenity, and apart also from the hideousness of the colours."

Beyond this, Orwell categorizes the postcards into rough themes, the most important of which are:

- Sex, which can be summarized in the knowledge that "Every man is plotting seduction and every woman is plotting marriage" and "Sex-appeal vanishes at about the age of twenty-five." This transitions rather neatly into:
- Home life, a shorthand for the fact that all marriages are miserable, which in turn explains why all middle-aged men are henpecked drunks.
- And then there's the obvious fact that toilets = hilarity.

The obscenity, he writes, is the whole point of them. These salty postcards occupied a unique niche in mid-twentieth-century Britain, a time and place where the censors decided on a regular basis what was moral and what was banned. Through some quirk of history, Donald McGill and his colleagues were permitted to bring their double (and more often single) entendres into the public sphere. Their work winked and nudged toward obvious jokes in a way that relieved some pressure.

Orwell's larger point is that society, then as now, asks a huge amount of us. And maybe after a bit of delay but always in the end, we deliver. We work hard, we fight wars, we take care of our children, we pay our taxes.

We will make the right decision, eventually—but please, just let us daydream what it might be like to stay home from work, to cheat on our spouses, to dodge the draft, to drink the day away, to shirk our duties. Let us at least consider taking a nap under the occasion rather than rising to it. And trust us to, having considered this temptation, deliver ourselves from it by ourselves.

Let us at least consider taking a nap under the occasion rather than rising to it.

Though he is withering in his analysis of the jokes—and in the process, proves that the dissection of a bad joke can be much funnier than the joke ever was—Orwell ultimately defends them as one of the few remaining outposts of a rich strain of British culture. His highest praise, which is utterly sincere, is that "in the past the mood of the comic postcard could enter into the central stream of literature, and jokes barely different from McGill's could casually be uttered between the murders in Shakespeare's tragedies. That is no longer possible, and a whole category of humor, integral to our literature till 1800 or thereabouts, has dwindled down to these ill-drawn postcards, leading a barely legal existence in cheap stationers' windows."

Orwell died in 1950, and in that same year Benny Hill made his first appearance on television. Hill's vaudeville-inspired shows were essentially Donald McGill postcards on the small screen, complete with lines like "She has a black belt in cookery. She can kill you with one chop" and "I'm not against half-naked girls. Not as often as I'd like to be." The salty humor may have gone underground for a century and a half, but it was definitely still there.

As the actor Michael Simkins put it in the *Telegraph* in 2011, "Sauce has long been the bedrock of both British humour and culinary heritage. From Chaucer, through Shakespeare and music hall to the Carry On films, a good sprinkling of innuendo has always been an essential ingredient of British comedy."

The primary ingredient in that sauce, of course, was salt.

TASTING NOTE: *TRUE DETECTIVE*

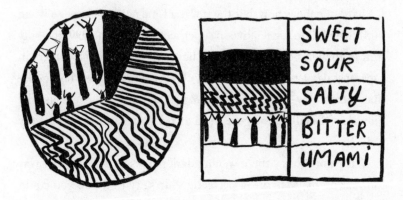

Sweet: 0 percent
Sour: 10 percent
Salty: 60 percent
Bitter: 30 percent
Umami: 0 percent

Upon its debut in 2014, HBO's detective series stood out because of its leading men, Matthew McConaughey and Woody Harrelson. But it really gained ground because while it had the intensity and darkness associated with just about every police procedural on television, it went even deeper with Rust Cohle's monologues on Christianity, the flat circle of time, nihilism, and the like. In short, it fused the expected saltiness with a rare strain of bitter. (It's unusual to find Nietzsche on television, even on premium cable.) Ultimately, the ending of season one wasn't nearly bitter enough for many, and the second season doubled down on the salt, ruining the dish.

Salty Superheroes

It's hard to believe now, but there was a time not too long ago when Hollywood didn't specialize in superhero movies. In 1999, the only film in the US box-office top one hundred to feature characters in capes was *Mystery Men*, a passingly clever parody of the whole genre that memorably featured a post-*Fargo* William H. Macy as The Shoveler ("Lucille, God gave me a gift. I shovel well. I shovel very well.")

That's not to say there weren't dark heroes on screen: That was the year of *The Matrix*—a perfectly sour-salty film—so you could argue that black leather trench coats were the capes of the time.

The X-Men series followed, and then Tobey Maguire's *Spider-Man*. The first was a surprisingly subtle parable about the struggle for gay rights, while the latter played up the weird things that happen to your body during adolescence (as portrayed by a twenty-seven-year-old). In other words, neither was particularly dark. And while both were hits, their influence was limited to air-conditioned cinemas in the summertime.

In 2005 came Christopher Nolan's *Batman Begins*, and with it a wave of dark, gritty, intense, comic-book films. They didn't even have to be based on comics, as franchises from James Bond to Planet of the Apes went dark. The supervillains in turn became not just diabolical but insane nihilists. The good guys became bad and the bad guys got even worse. The soundtracks were powered by electro-foghorns. And the jokes were in short supply.

The natural end point would seem to be Zack Snyder's *Man of Steel*, the original hero and also one of the silliest. To make Superman dark, the costume notably replaced the red underwear with a monotone body suit, because, as the director explained, "I couldn't make it consistent with the world that we were creating."

What happened in that time was that superhero films shifted from sour to salty, with the previously noted exception of the Marvel movies, kicked off by *Iron Man* in 2008. (The studio's most convincing foray into the saline has been *Deadpool*, which earns its R rating but keeps the salt and the sour in equal proportion.) The audience discovered a new taste for salty heroes, and Hollywood doubled down.

And that seems like what these movies are going to be for the near future: Sweet-sour or very salty, or some winning combination of those two. As long as the recipe keeps being adjusted—not so silly that it alienates the fans, not so serious that it confuses those who still expect their comic books to be slightly comical— there's no sign that it will end any time soon. Just as there's a Lex Luthor for every Superman, the constant balance of lovable Marvel heroes to morose every-other-heroes seems to keep everyone happy.

Well, not everyone; there are some moviegoers who, for some antiquated reason, don't want all their films to be epic franchises based on comic books. For them, there was *Birdman, or The Unexpected Virtue of Ignorance*, which added bitterness to the superhero formula, brought back the original big-screen Batman and could be viewed as Hollywood wondering how, if ever, it will get out from under the capes. But the fans want what they want, and though *Birdman* was 2014's best picture, that year's real superhero surprise was the unlikely success of *Guardians of the Galaxy*, a third-tier franchise silly enough to feature a talking tree hero. More sweet, less salt.

The next step of superhero evolution seems clear: a franchise that combines *The Avengers'* sweetness, *Iron Man*'s sourness, *The Dark Knight*'s saltiness, *Birdman*'s bitterness, and some magical additional dash of umami. Ketchup Man, the audiences are waiting.

TASTING NOTE: DRAKE AND THE WEEKND

Drake:
Sweet: 20 percent
Sour: 20 percent
Salty: 50 percent
Bitter: 5 percent
Umami: 5 percent

The Weeknd:
Sweet: 10 percent
Sour: 20 percent
Salty: 60 percent
Bitter: 5 percent
Umami: 5 percent

Aubrey Drake Graham started out as sweet as can be: a child actor who portrayed a wheelchair-bound teen on a Canadian television drama. His transformation into a rap star blended some of that sweetness—the sweaters, the goofy dancing, the big smile—with a whole lot of salt. Hedonism, self-pity, and jealousy are his main themes, and they're only amplified by his protégé Abel Tesfaye, aka The Weeknd. Both are obsessed with how bad they are and how badly they've been treated. Tesfaye wrote an all-ages chart topper about the side effects of cocaine, an irony he reflects on in the song "Reminder": "I just won a new award for a kids' show / Talkin' 'bout a face numbing off a bag of blow." Drake is more likely to shout out to soft drinks than hard drugs, but both base their personas on an unabashed, immodest saltiness.

Disco Won

On July 12, 1979, you could watch the Chicago White Sox host the Detroit Tigers in a doubleheader for just ninety-eight cents— provided you brought a record to be destroyed. That's how Disco Demolition Night started.

Comiskey Park could hold fifty thousand people. Ninety thousand showed up, climbing the fences to get in. When the local DJ who came up with the idea detonated a crate of records between games, a fire started and he fled the diamond.

Fans responded by charging the field, whipping records through the air. They set more fires and ripped down the batting cage. Chicago police arrested thirty-nine people and the second game was forfeited.

It's now remembered in one of two ways: as a silly night when music fans finally put an end to the plague of disco beats that were

threatening rock 'n' roll's rightful place at the heart of American music, or as tragic evidence of a racist and homophobic mob revolting against a genre that celebrated cosmopolitan inclusivity.

Those who remember it as an artifact of the ridiculous 1970s, like the Pet Rock and the leisure suit, are clear that it was just about the music. Those who see it as something altogether darker are equally clear that it was really about what the music represented.

To these two interpretations, let us add a third: rock vs. disco was really sour vs. salty. Rock is thrilling, rebellious, and adolescent; Disco is edgy, immodest, and hedonistic. They didn't mix—at least in the beginning.

Compare 1979's top two songs in the US on the Billboard charts. Number one was "My Sharona" by the Knack, as pure an expression of inarticulate teenage longing as anything in pop music; as singer Doug Fieger told the *Washington Post* in 1995, "It's just an honest song about a fourteen-year-old boy."

The runner-up was "Bad Girls" by Donna Summer. Produced by Giorgio Moroder, it was inspired by the rage Summer felt when a Los Angeles police officer mistook one of her assistants—a black woman in business attire—for a prostitute. Also, the song's oft-sampled "toot toot" and "beep beep" lyrics represent the car horns of men soliciting sex.

If there is one lesson to be learned about the last days of disco, it's that they will never arrive. Disco lost the battle but fought back with guerrilla tactics to win the war. Or as John Seabrook wrote in *The Song Machine*, his 2015 book on how pop music gets made: "I thought disco was dead. Turns out disco had simply gone underground, where it became House, only to eventually reemerge, cicadalike, as the backing track to the [contemporary hit radio] music and to bludgeon rock senseless with synths."

The synthesizers, the drugs, the inclusive nature of the music—these scattered out to different parts of the culture, into hundreds of subcultures and thousands of songs. Disco became techno, dance, hip-hop, house, etc. Every pop song in the 1980s that used a synthesizer—in other words, every pop song in the 1980s—owed something to disco. Consider the long life of Chic's "Good Times," which topped the Billboard Hot 100 in 1979 but has been continually sampled since, most famously as the backing track for "Rapper's Delight" by the Sugarhill Gang and most repeatedly by Daft Punk.

The good news is that this sort of taste battle royale is unlikely to ever happen again. What happened at Comiskey Park was a battle over who got to control the megaphone of mainstream culture. Someone always had to be a loser in the monoculture, and in 1979 the losers were the people who didn't want their radio station to run a Donna Summer marathon. Nowadays, you can stream as much Donna as you need for pennies on the dollar. Everyone's individual taste can be satisfied. (Even if it turns out that when presented with infinite variety, most of us still pick the mainstream hits.)

Culture is no longer winner-takes-all, and despite whatever nostalgia may exist for the (somewhat fictional) days when we all loved the same movies and sang along to the same songs, it's a horrible way to program a radio station. There surely was hate directed at disco, but some of that had to come from the simple frustration of trying and failing to find the music you grew up with on the radio.

With the end of that problem and the intermingling of popular music, it seems that fans of the sour actually appreciate the salty. The French robots of Daft Punk worked with Giorgio Moroder to "Get Lucky," and if you attend a wedding in the next decade, you'll almost certainly dance to Bruno Mars's "Uptown Funk." Disco rocks, and few wars have been won so decisively.

TASTING NOTE: TREY PARKER AND MATT STONE

Sweet: 5 percent
Sour: 10 percent
Salty: 50 percent
Bitter: 30 percent
Umami: 5 percent

Matt and Trey are a duo like salt and pepper, only they're salt and salt. Their first movie was *Cannibal! The Musical*, a story of the ill-fated Packer expedition and the instigator of a thousand *Exclamation Point! The Musical* plays at fringe festivals. They created *South Park*. They forced the Motion Picture Association of America to censor puppet sex in *Team America: World Police*. They won Tonys for *The Book of Mormon*. And they did it all because they realized a little bit too much salt can be the best way to deliver a sophisticated message.

Or as Stone told MTV's Kurt Loder in an interview about *Team*

America: "[Being offensive is] what's funny. And that's almost the only way you can make people think about anything anymore. The culture is just so coarse that you have to take it to that level and people will be like, 'Whoa!' And then you can make people think about stuff. It's kind of like shock therapy."

This is indisputably true. It's what Joyce did with *Ulysses*. It's what Nabokov did with *Lolita*. And it's what Cyrus did with "Wrecking Ball."

Salty–Sweet: So Wrong but So Right

No taste combination is as wrong in theory and as right in practice as sweet and salty. Chocolate-covered potato chips, honey-roasted peanuts, melon wrapped in prosciutto, Chicago-style cheese and caramel popcorn, and sea-salt dark chocolate all have their devotees. Collections of salty/sweet recipes encourage cooks to "cover all the bases" (Martha Stewart), "have it both ways" (Health.com), and "Embrace the salt, because life is so much sweeter when you do" (Food52). And indeed, there is scientific proof that salt elevates sweetness and suppresses bitterness, which is why some eccentric breakfasters will sprinkle it on their grapefruit.

A little bit of salt makes sweet things sweeter.

The technical term for this is mutual suppression. As one research paper explained it, "Salt enhanced sweetness at low concentrations." In other words, a little bit of salt makes sweet things sweeter.

No less an authority than Nigella Lawson

traced the so-wrong-but-so-right combination back to the Brittany region of France, already famous for its salted butter. From there, she writes, it inspired pastry chef Pierre Hermé's salted caramel macaron in the 1990s, and from there the salted sweetness trend trickled into the mainstream. And who better to champion the mix of sweet (uncomplicated, pleasant, popular) and salty (immodest, hedonistic, experienced) than Nigella herself? Just consider how she describes her first encounter with salted caramel:

"Not since the first ever infant suckled at its mother's breast had a food—it felt—had so much instant impact. If I'd been in a cartoon, my eyes would have bulged, stars would have emanated from my head, and I would have been licking my saliva-spurting lips wolfishly." She describes how her "love affair" is "heady, it's passionate" and that when you add fat to the combination, it's "not so much a pairing, but a rapturous ménage à trois."

This description of sweetness and salt is both sweet and salty, and thus makes Lawson the perfect cultural embodiment of the flavor pairing. The *Guardian* describes her appeal as a combination of "licked fingers, obliviously amused dinner party guests and thousands of steaming, unctuous, overflowing, blisteringly unnecessary adjectives." She's safe enough for a daytime cooking show, but much more suggestive than, say, Rachael Ray.

For total mainstream acceptance of sweet-salty, you need only turn on the radio. What was once called top forty is now known as CHR—contemporary hits radio—and when it's most effective, it's both sweet enough to attract you to its hooks and then (when you actually listen to the lyrics) salty enough to shock anyone old enough to remember when obscenity was still an issue debated in public.

John Seabrook describes being introduced to this genre by his son: "The music reminded me a little of the bubblegum pop of my preteen years, but it was vodka-flavored and laced with MDMA; it doesn't taste like 'Sugar, Sugar.' It is teen pop for adults."

And, eventually, he comes to like it. Though he admits that, like "snack food, it leaves you feeling unsatisfied, always craving just a little more."

The apogee of sweet-salty pop is Katy Perry, who Seabrook accurately describes as "part Playboy bunny and part Little Bo Peep." Perry famously grew up in a house so religious that they called devilled eggs "angel eggs," and began her music career as a gospel singer. But then she kissed a girl, duetted with a leering Snoop Dogg on "California Gurls," and became a heroine to tweens with the empowerment anthem "Roar."

Perry walks the line like no one else in popular culture, and the result is that she is beloved by a very specific demographic. As James Parker wrote about Nickelodeon and the Disney Channel's endless string of preteen sitcoms in the *Atlantic*: "Indeed, the voice of Katy Perry, huge and exhortatory, as if running for office or declaring war, seems to roll through all these shows. Power is her theme, every Katy Perry fan a kind of private banana republic of self-affirmation— You're gonna hear me ro-OOOAR!—and power is the major trope of today's tweencom."

This power is entirely in her mastery of the sweet and the salty, sexuality just wholesome enough to be sold at Walmart. Just like Nigella Lawson, Katy Perry has helpfully underlined this metaphor with an actual foodstuff. As part of her endorsement of popchips and investment in the company, the snack food brand came out with Katy's Kettle Corn flavor, designed to fulfill the singer's desire for "a little bit of sweet and a little bit of salt."

Palate Cleanser

The Impossibility of Bad Taste

B ad taste is a nice idea, a clean category, and a convenient fiction. For it to exist, we would need universal preferences, an agreed-upon societal standard and a commitment to accepting it without questioning. We'd all have to pretend we were born in the same country at the same time, attended the same schools, had the same friends, and enjoyed the same things. It wouldn't make any sense, but we'd also all have to agree not to point that out. For large swaths of human history, this has actually been the state of affairs.

It was the case on November 13, 1959, in Cleveland Heights, Ohio. It was on that date that the Heights Art Theater screened Louis Malle's *The Lovers*, a French film about that most French of subjects, adultery. Spoiler alert: The affair is consummated, and the actress Jeanne Moreau is depicted in orgasmic rapture. The sex scene is unambiguous but leaves almost everything to the imagination—specifically, the imaginations of Cleveland Heights detective Earl Gordon and his wife, Doris. The couple attended the screening because theater owner Nico Jacobellis had been unable, or perhaps unwilling, to let the local constabulary review the film before it opened. Detective Gordon described the movie to his superiors, and the next night the county prosecutor and the city's law director accompanied him to the film. They sat through the first screening before they took action, shutting down the second screening, confiscating all five canisters of film, and arresting the theater owner. The charge was obscenity, which was very vaguely defined by a 231-word state law.

Jacobellis fought the case all the way to the US Supreme Court, where the justices overturned his conviction but couldn't agree on any other part of the case. In fact, among the nine judges there were seven opinions. (That's what happens when you try to legislate taste.) And this is where the possibility of a rational determination of taste found its most cogent (and still utterly lacking) defense. In the words of Justice Potter Stewart:

> *It is possible to read the Court's opinion in Roth v. United States and Alberts v. California, 354 U. S. 476, in a variety of ways. In saying this, I imply no criticism of the Court, which in those cases was faced with the task of trying to define what may be indefinable. I have reached the conclusion, which I think is confirmed at least by negative implication in the Court's decisions since Roth and Alberts, that under the First and Fourteenth Amendments criminal laws in this area are constitutionally limited to hard-core pornography. I shall not today attempt further to define the kinds of material I understand to be embraced within that shorthand description; and perhaps I could never succeed in intelligibly doing so. But I know it when I see it, and the motion picture involved in this case is not that.*

His famous nondescriptive description of hard-core pornography—"I know it when I see it"—is a perfect dodge. The offending matter here is essentially Cleveland Heights's epitome of bad taste, the thing so abhorrent to the community that they needed to go to the highest court in the land to protect their right to ban it. But Stewart pinpoints the problem with this case not in his most famous line but the one slightly before it, when he describes the court as being "faced with the task of trying to define what may be indefinable."

That is the thing about bad taste. Knowing it when you see it means that we always need the "you" in that sentence by our sides, whispering catty comments in our ears. "That's a provocative film, but it's not pornography." *Thanks, Justice Stewart!* "This meal is decent, but I've had better." *I'll pick another restaurant next time, Justice Stewart!* "She really shouldn't be wearing those pants." *Shh, Justice Stewart! She can totally hear your stage whisper!*

This is impractical, not least because Potter Stewart died in 1985.

Five years later, Jane and Michael Stern published *The Encyclopedia of Bad Taste*. The coffee-table book is filled with entries on subjects like bumper stickers, heavy metal, poodles, and tattoos. How did the authors select the entries? As they explain in the introduction, bad taste is what is inappropriate. Bad taste "tries too hard to mirror good taste and winds up like Alice through the looking glass, on the wrong side." It "frequently tries to improve on nature." It "has mischievous appeal because it breaks rules and flouts decorum."

They don't come right out and say it, but their rule of thumb appears to be that bad taste is inauthentic. So then maybe good taste is authenticity? But that then requires a definition of "authentic," which is a lot like trying to define taste. You know what authenticity is when you see it.

The Encyclopedia of Bad Taste is a product of its time. It usefully corrects Pierre Bourdieu's rich snobs vs. poor slobs thinking by pointing out that "the equation between class and taste is not so tidy." And it hints at what's to come: "When things hang around this collective cultural Warehouse of the Damned long enough, they begin to shimmy with a kind of newfound energy and fascination."

Eventually, cultural norms shift and bad taste becomes good. In enough time, "it might just happen to everything in this encyclopedia."

It's been more than a quarter century, so we've been given time—but something else has happened since the years of the first Bush administration. Back then, as Doc Brown explains to Marty in *Back to the Future*, cultural time was linear. In 1990, everyone watched *Cheers* on Thursday nights, and you could probably hum a few bars of "Hold On" by Wilson Phillips. But with the advent of digital culture and the slow decay of the mainstream, there was no overwhelming consensus on what to like.

You can plot this quite dramatically in the percentage audience share of TV's biggest finales. In 1983, 77 percent of viewers watched the *M*A*S*H* finale. In 1993, 64 percent watched the *Cheers* finale. In 1998, 58 percent watched the *Seinfeld* finale. In 2004, 43 percent watched the *Friends* finale. No finale since then has cracked the top ten most-watched finales—ten times more people watched the last episode of *M*A*S*H* than the finales of *The Sopranos*, *Sex and the City*, or *Breaking Bad*. (Though, to be fair, not a single *M*A*S*H* viewer live tweeted the last episode.) We're watching more TV than ever before, but we're all watching different things at different times.

Kurt Andersen put his finger on this in a 2012 *Vanity Fair* essay, in which he began by noticing that what was stylish in 2012 was essentially identical to what was stylish in 1992. Part of his reasoning was that technology had taken the place of culture as the place we look for what's new. And part of it was that culture had become fully democratized. "Tastefulness scales," as he put it. And that scale had created a culture where it is both effortless to be generically tasteful—just shop at IKEA—and only slightly more work to be uniquely so—scour Craigslist for some midcentury modern knockoffs.

In this world, it's much more helpful to think about taste as something you either have or you don't. If you don't, chances are you blend in just fine. You just select the defaults. You buy decent clothes, listen to decent music, eat decent food, and never need worry that any of these things will be included in what today would be called the Wikipedia of Bad Taste.

If you do have taste, then you can source a Polymer Records T-shirt that refers to the fictional record label from the classic 1984 rockumentary *This Is Spinal Tap*. It's available from Last Exit to Nowhere, a British company that specializes in clothing featuring fictional brands from popular culture, and it'll run you about $40, including shipping.

The difference between these two ways of living is that the first was the path of least resistance, while the second required some thought. It's the progression from zero to one.

There is one gray area in this black-and-white definition,

however. If taste is making a choice and tastelessness is just taking what's in front of you, what happens if you make a choice to just take what's in front of you? What if you *really* like shopping at IKEA?

Two buzzwords of the same recent vintage aim to describe this phenomenon of choosing not to be choosy. There's "basic," a dismissive adjective usually applied to women, and "normcore," a movement labeled by the trend-forecasting group K-Hole in 2014.

> *To be basic is to be undemanding of the world.*

To be basic is to be undemanding of the world. The adjective is an insult, and it is almost always paired with "bitch." There are no basic bros, though it could be argued that all bros are basic. (Except the bronies.) To distill the Internet's countless essays and lists on the subject of basic, it means you like pumpkin spice lattes, yoga pants, and *Sex and the City*. You are a conformist consumer. In the viral words of preteen Internet celebrity Lohanthony, "A basic bitch would have to be someone who does what everyone else is doing and isn't their own person at all." (Note that Lohanthony describes himself as "far from normal, I promise, and I choose to celebrate that"—so essentially, antibasic.)

To be normcore is to be basic for a higher purpose. The K-Hole paper that coined the term also discusses Acting Basic, Youth Mode, and Mass Indie, and is so gnomic in its pronouncements that it was immediately misinterpreted. (In the trendcasting business, as in all genres of fortune-telling, the vaguest predictions are the most likely to come true.) As the company explains, "normcore finds liberation in being nothing special, and realizes that adaptability leads to belonging." It's about a "post-authenticity coolness that opts into sameness." It's "a path to a more peaceful life." And it means that when you order a pumpkin spice latte, it's not because "you're not your own person," but because "one does not pretend to be above the indignity of belonging" to a seasonal coffee promotion. Or to put it another way, you are comfortable enough in who you are that you don't need a beverage to signal that to the world.

So how can you tell them apart? Intention, in theory. Was the choice mindless or mindful? Tasteless or tasteful? Who cares? Sometimes a latte is just a latte.

In practice, this is a distinction without a difference. Whether we're being basic or normcore, on occasion we all choose to go with the flow. Take a break. Order combo number one. Drive the bestselling car in America. Turn on the radio. There are thousands of daily choices to make in a consumer society, most of them meaningless, so by all means exercise your right to opt out. Don't taste, just be. And know that eventually, you'll encounter something you want to keep encountering—or permanently avoid. Maybe you don't like that particular blend of cinnamon, nutmeg, and allspice. Maybe the cinnamon dolce latte is more your speed. And before you know it, you're back to the Elements of Taste.

5

Bitter: The Taste of Repulsion

Featuring: The First, Second, and Third Waves of
Coffee, Interpersonal Chemistry through
Negativity, *Meek's Cutoff*, and the Opposite of
Industrial Lighting

You are not supposed to like bitter foods. The whole point of them is to drive you away. Poison can take many forms, but more often than not it tastes bitter. Just as we need sweet, sour, and salty taste buds to find the good stuff, we need bitter buds to escape the bad. During Passover, Jews eat bitter herbs to remind themselves of their ancestors' suffering.

And yet it says something about our species that a sizeable portion of us actually like bitter tastes. We take a technique used to preserve ale on long ocean voyages and make it the top-selling style of craft beer. We seek out arugula when romaine lettuce is cheaper and more palatable. We buy chocolate that's so dark, the bar is just acrid brown dust in a plastic tray. Yecch.

You are not supposed to like bitter culture. (Note: The following paragraph will be simplistic, reductive, and ignorant of anything other than the here and now.) Ballet, opera, poetry, literary fiction, art-house film, modern art: none of these things qualify as, you know, popular. If opera were designed to be immediately accessible, it wouldn't consist of convoluted plots (strike one) or sung (strike two) in Italian (strike three) over many hours (strike four) in elite venues (strike five) at a relatively high cost to attendees (strike six). But every metropolis in the world that aspires to be world-class has an opera house, and those that really want to run with the big dogs know that opera house has to have hosted a complete performance of Wagner's *Ring Cycle*, the opera that makes other operas look like Marvel movies. *Der Ring des Nibelungen* adds to the bitterness of its art form by stretching over four nights (strike seven), requiring a gigantic cast and orchestra (strike eight), and being a personal favorite of Adolf Hitler (You're out).

And yet: our definition of cultural ketchup—the ideal work of art that blends all the tastes in perfect harmony—is what Wagner called the *Gesamtkunstwerk*: the work of art that would synthesize the best of all previous works. Every bit of Nordic myth (plus some of his own invention), from the beginning of the world to the Twilight of the Gods, finds its way into the cycle.

It has, of course, become freighted with the admiration and scorn of its many admirers and detractors. And while its universality is a given, it certainly reflects the time and place of its creation. So it was inevitable that even a *Gesamtkunstwerk* would be sampled and remixed by artists hoping to add a dash of immortality to their work. Which brings us to *Star Wars*: drawing from myth, conceived as an epic, revolving around the light vs. dark, featuring separated-at-birth twins who (to differing degrees) fall in love. Regardless of how you feel about Jar-Jar Binks, there is no denying that George Lucas created a modern myth. And he began with bitterness.

So why do we like things that are bitter? Maybe, like Homer Simpson upon learning that Marge has purchased tickets to the ballet, we simply don't know what we're in for.

"The ballet? Woo-hoo!"
"You like ballet?"
"Marjorie, please! I enjoy all the meats of our cultural stew!
      Ah, ballet!"
(Imagines a trained bear driving a small car in circles)

But even Homer realizes the truth soon enough.

In her cookbook devoted exclusively to bitterness, Jennifer McLagan talks to a food scientist who explains that bitter "conveys a very simple hedonic message—if excessive, don't consume." Fittingly for bitterness, that may make it the perfect taste for our times. Instead of throwing itself at you with a never-ending stream of pickup lines, this is a taste that's playing hard to get. You're going to have to put in a bit of effort to like bitter things. And as the effort we put into a task generally correlates to the satisfaction we derive from it, we can end up liking bitterness after all. That's how we acquire an acquired taste. And that's why the above tirade against opera just skips along the surface of a shallow argument.

The physical taste of bitterness is hard to identify. As McLagan writes, "while only acids signal 'sour,' by contrast thousands of different compounds in foods elicit a 'bitter' response." And we can sense bitterness by "smell, temperature, color, texture, and how the food feels in our mouth," as well as "a whole range of cultural, environmental, experiential, and genetic factors." Again, if sweet and salty are flashing LED signs at the front of the grocery store, bitter is a mildly revolting smell emanating from a half-open closet behind the produce department. And still we search it out.

Why? One evolutionary theory has it that bitter foods remind us of hard times, and so hard times have us reaching for bitter foods. As explained in a 2012 paper, the crops we eat become bitter when they're subjected to drought or floods. If our predecessors were to survive, they had to develop a taste for these dying plants. "There is likely co-evolution of a human taste for bitterness and a motivation and mental preparedness to survive hard times," write Bin-Bin Chen and Lei Chang in the *Journal of Experimental Social Psychology*. The implication there is that the brothers and sisters of our ancestors who refused to eat bitter foods didn't get a chance to pass along their genes. And they extrapolate that theory one step further by suggesting that the reason we drink coffee and tea is not just the caffeine but rather the bitter taste we seek when our bodies tell us we are tired—this, they claim, explains decaf. Bitterness builds character; by this definition, it's a bad taste with good implications.

Bitterness builds character.

McLagan's cookbook notes that "[W]ithout a touch of bitterness, your cooking will be lacking a dimension. Furthermore, bitter is both an appetite stimulant and a digestive—that is, it has the power to make you hungry as well as helping you digest your meal." No matter how we came to appreciate bitterness, it is a taste we can appreciate. Not at first, not with ease, and generally not in isolation—cream and sugar in your coffee?—but we do.

Coffee, Beer, and Cults of Bitterness

> Coffee is a much more powerful stimulant than is believed. A strong man can live a long time and still drink two bottles of wine every day. The same man could not support a like quantity of coffee; he would become imbecilic, or would die of consumption.
> —JEAN ANTHELME BRILLAT-SAVARIN, THE PHYSIOLOGY OF TASTE

While it's true that bitterness suggests poison and that we instinctively avoid bitter foods, it's also true that some of the world's most popular beverages are bitter. Coffee, tea, and beer are all naturally this way—which is why few people drink them straight. The default is cream in your coffee, sugar in your tea, and—for fans of mass-produced lagers—water in your beer.

That said, there is a sizeable (and vocal!) minority that likes to keep these bitter drinks bitter. The bitter lovers appreciate their India Pale Ales and their espresso, and they rose in tandem with the famous Three Waves of Coffee. This theory of coffee consumption refers to the US in the twentieth century, and it was first developed by Trish Skeie in a 2003 article for the *Flamekeeper*, the newsletter of the Roasters Guild, an arm of the Specialty Coffee Association of America.

The First Wavers are the people who made coffee both the best part of waking up and good to the last drop. "We like to point at them and say: look who made bad coffee commonplace, look who created low-quality instant solubles, look who blended away all the nuance, look who forced prices to an all-time low!" Skeie writes, but she defends these grandfathers of caffeination. "Airtight cans, pre-ground portion packs, and Juan Valdez were their ideas."

Then came the Second Wavers, among whom Skeie counts herself: "Whether we began our careers in the late '60s or mid-1990s, we tend to have a common philosophy. Our entrance was artisan driven. Someone turned us on to coffee origins and roasting styles."

The Second Wave washed into every airport lounge, every shopping mall, and every upscale neighborhood in the form of Starbucks. So synonymous is the green siren logo with gentrification that a study by the real-estate site Zillow claimed a correlation between long-term home values and proximity to a Frappuccino vendor. There are now more than twenty thousand Starbucks locations in the world; when Skeie was considering the Second Wave, she noted that they didn't try to hide their ambitious goal of "two thousand outlets by the year 2000."

The connoisseur's reaction was the Third Wave. Whereas the Second Wave took the mass production of the First Wave and dramatically increased the quality, the Third Wave consciously discards all that industrialized perfection. Third Wave coffee is hand-pulled shots and pour-over drip, prepared while you wait. (Indeed, you're paying for the wait.) And the right way to make it is entirely up to the barista.

"A Third Waver's opinion is a constant work in progress," Skeie remarks. "There are as many extraction truths as there are espressos. The variables are endless with coffee, and this is what they are teaching their staff and customers."

These Waves, moving from awareness to improvement to personalization, are reminiscent of social movements ranging from
feminism to capitalism. With each step,
the people who really, truly like the
taste of coffee have it a little bit better.
First, they could buy drinkable coffee
in the grocery store; then, they could
get palatable espresso in the bookstore; and now they can explore rare
varietals in just about every trendy
neighborhood in the Western world.

Starbucks does a decent job of trying to contain all the waves.
You can find Clover coffee (a sort of upside-down French press) in
many of their stores, as well as light roasts for the Folgers set and a
whole range of milkshakes that have only a passing resemblance to
coffee.

But for those who appreciate coffee's aesthetic bitterness, this
will never suffice. The beverage can be bitter in the sense of being demanding, cultured, and hard to like—and like anything bitter, the
more of it you try, the more you're willing to try. And in that way,
while the First and Second Waves were always about the economics
of selling more coffee to more people, they also had the effect of
making a sizeable portion of the population like more extreme forms
of the beverage and go to more extreme lengths to get it.

And at about the same time that the Third Wave of Coffee began,
there was a serious schism in the beer world. The craft movement had
begun, and around North America small breweries were experi-
menting with flavor and finding willing test subjects. Like coffee,
there were endless variables to examine. The beer snob has much in

common with the coffee geek, and the origins of their passions are in-structive. Both are made, not born, and exactly how this happens for coffee helps explain how all cults of bitterness come to be.

Sociologist John Manzo has studied the coffee subculture, and among his findings is the observation that these geeks were not born into good beans. "In fact," Manzo writes, "one persistent statement concerns how dreadful users' parents' tastes in coffee were, and how they sometimes, in a manner completely at odds with the notion of taste being an ascribed characteristic, manage to teach their parents about the vagaries of quality coffee."

It's hard work for them to source, prepare, and enjoy coffee that meets the standards they've elevated for themselves. And worse yet, this insistence on top-quality coffee costs them socially. By culti-vating a taste for the bitter, they become less pleasant for the Maxwell House–bound to be around. As one coffee geek says, "My coffee obsession seems to be destroying part of my social life. If I say, 'Let's get together over coffee,' the person seems terrified that I'm going to judge them for ordering a caramel macchiato."

And that terror may not be unfounded. Take this self-reported conversation between a coffee snob couple:

Her: "You know, there just don't seem to be enough places where we can go and get a bad espresso."

Him: "I've noticed that too. I actually saw a corner in town where there wasn't a Starbucks."

Her: "Maybe you should see if there's a shop there for lease and you could open a coffee shop."

Him: "I don't know. I'm not very good at making bad
espresso. And my drinks . . . you can actually taste
the coffee in it, and a lot of people don't like that."

Just picturing these two smugly sipping their cappuccinos may
leave a taste worse than a caramel praline latte in many mouths. At
least they found each other. And of course, he also found an Internet
forum where he could share this conversation and roll his eyes at the
masses with a small group of like-minded people.

(It also brings to mind the aforementioned research paper with
the to-the-point title "Bitter Taste Causes Hostility," and its finding
that "the intake of a bitter substance caused participants to harm another person by attributing less competency and friendliness . . .
even substances consumed in everyday life make people more hostile
toward others." Despite their "Give Me Coffee and Nobody Gets
Hurt" novelty mugs, though, reports of widespread Third Wave
coffee geek violence are lacking.)

Craft beer isn't better beer so much as it's a different beverage,
and most beer snobs will grudgingly admit that the megabrewers
are remarkably consistent and effective at producing perfectly boring
pilsners. As Sam Calagione, the brewer behind Dogfish Head and
one of the leaders of the craft revolution, told the *New Yorker* in
2008:

"I'm not afraid to pay compliments where compliments are due.
Anheuser-Busch's quality—if quality is consistency—is second to
none. But I'm frustrated that that one beer has been hammered
down people's throats. I mean, banana cream pie may be your favorite fucking food. But if you ate banana cream pie every day you
would hate it too."

The larger finding here is the interwoven appeal of both hating things other people like and liking things other people hate. And, to take it a step further, there is the dark appeal of bonding by exclusion. Craft beer snobs who enjoy hopped-up IPAs and those who prefer Belgian tripel ales like very different things, though they may both hate Bud. Or as psychologist Jennifer Bosson puts it in her paper "Interpersonal Chemistry Through Negativity," bonding over things you hate "establishes in-group/out-group boundaries, boosts self-esteem, and conveys highly diagnostic information about attitude holders." And this effect goes both ways: consider Budweiser's 2016 Super Bowl ad, which proclaimed their beer was "Not a Hobby. Not Small. Not Sipped. Not Soft. Not Imported. Not a Fruit Cup. Not Following. Not for Everyone."

Ultimately, though, you're the one sipping the coffee, drinking the beer, watching the opera, or reading the poem. What makes that bitterness worthwhile?

In all cases, the thrill of the hunt cannot be underestimated. You didn't drink the first thing they served you; you put effort into the search for something different. Perhaps it was something off the beaten path, something no one expected you to enjoy. Is it empirically better? It doesn't matter. Your satisfaction is informed by the rewards of your work, and as everyone knows, getting there is half the fun. Especially if the coffee's hot upon your arrival.

TASTING NOTE: TIM AND ERIC

Sweet: 0 percent
Sour: 0 percent
Salty: 20 percent
Bitter: 80 percent
Umami: 0 percent

The best explanation of what Tim Heidecker and Eric Wareheim's work is comes from an online compilation of what it isn't. Not Tim and Eric, a subreddit forum devoted to videos that match the comedy duo's lo-fi aesthetic, specifically excludes their actual sketches. Instead, the content guide explains that because their anti-humor "relies on awkward presentation to overstimulate and/or unseat their audience," this is the place to share genuinely awkward content seen on public-access television and elsewhere. (The difference between genuine and deliberate awkwardness is like the difference between seeing a work of conceptual art in a white-walled gallery or in a Dumpster: entirely a question of context.) To enjoy being "unseated" is to enjoy bitterness. To enjoy their comedy, you have to both recognize how awkward it is and embrace that awkwardness. If you watch enough of Tim and Eric's minimalist highlighting of reality—or, for that matter, Andy Kaufman's stand-up from a generation before—you can end up seeing the entire world as an infinitely subtle, totally subversive joke. (Which you can then post to reddit.) As far as coping strategies for modern life go, it's not a bad one.

Unwatchable Films

Meek's Cutoff is a 2010 film by the director Kelly Reichardt that, in the words of Roger Ebert, "evokes what must have been the reality of wagon trains to the West. They were grueling, dirty, thirsty, burning and freezing ordeals." In his three-and-a-half-star review, Ebert writes that Reichardt "doesn't make it easy for us with simplistic character conflict," focusing instead on "misery and exhaustion."

Writing in the *New York Times Magazine*, Dan Kois agreed with Ebert: The movie was in fact "as closed off and stubborn as the devout settlers who populate it." For what it is, it is well done. But why would anyone want to watch what it is? "As I get older, I find I'm suffering from a kind of culture fatigue and have less interest in eating my cultural vegetables, no matter how good they may be for me," Kois writes.

The reaction this set off was immediate and intense: It was the "moronic yet well-circulated" and "dispiriting" work of a "self-indulgent infant." Both of the *Times*'s chief film critics fired back in paired essays under the headline "In Defense of the Slow and the Boring." Manohla Dargis writes of the value in not being entertained in a movie; of being allowed to let your mind wander, or even to think. And she points out Andy Warhol's description of true cultural fatigue being what you experience when you see "the same plots and the same shots and the same cuts over and over again."

A. O. Scott is slightly more forgiving, and he returns to the vegetable metaphor, writing that "I would like to think there is room in the cinematic diet for various flavors, including some that may seem, on first encounter, unfamiliar or even unpleasant."

The physical taste to cultural metaphor is rarely so clear, and so a simple reframing of the problem makes the solution obvious. Once you become an adult, you can choose what vegetables you want to eat. If you want to specifically avoid rapini, you can still live a full, rich life. Avoiding all veggies and eating only breakfast cereal may be too extreme. Subsisting entirely on dandelion greens seems like a bad idea, unless you're some sort of monk. Or on a doomed wagon train.

TASTING NOTE: KANYE WEST

Sweet: 0 percent
Sour: 10 percent
Salty: 40 percent
Bitter: 40 percent
Umami: 10 percent

If the bitter is that which is hard to like, can there be any more enthusiastic spokesman for the flavor than Kanye West? Here is an artist who will do whatever it takes to be disliked—or perhaps he's so true to his creative vision that he doesn't pause to consider the feelings of his fans, his enemies, or Taylor Swift? He's self-aware enough to record a song about how those who miss the old Kanye should remember that he invented Kanye and spawned a legion of imitators, and then note how Kanye it would be if Kanye sang about missing the old Kanye. Is this clever artistic license or self-obsessed swagger? As Kanye is equal parts between salty and bitter, he gets to have it both ways and his way.

When Bitter Is Better

The word "luxury" is rapidly catching up with "classy" as the sort of description that, if used in a sentence, negates the intended effect. Real luxury doesn't use the term "luxury": it's like screaming about how quiet you are.

Luxury does serve a real economic purpose, though, beyond just enabling conspicuous consumption by signaling who will be first against the wall when the revolution comes. Car companies, for instance, justify the drastic markups on their luxury fleets by coming up with new bells and whistles every year. These eventually trickle down to even the discount models, which is why there are airbags in your hatchback. This isn't altruism on anyone's part, but merely a way to get the executive who wants the nicest car in the company parking lot to pay more so the cheap cars can be even cheaper.

Research into what defines luxury has identified six main factors:

1. It's a high-quality product or experience
2. That costs significantly more than it needs to
3. With a satisfying production story
4. Available in limited quantities
5. Offered with personalization
6. That separates you from the crowd.

This describes your Rolex or your Ferrari, but also, to some degree, your organic kale or your subscription to a weekend newspaper. It's not enough to say it's simply the best, because much of what Costco sells may qualify by at least some metric as "the best" though no one buys luxury in a warehouse. It is both a reward for yourself and a signal to others.

The easiest way to duck the question of taste is to simply insist on quality. That's what Oscar Wilde did when asked what he might like for dinner: "Oh, anything. Anything, no matter what. I have the simplest tastes. I am always satisfied with the best." A similar story was later told of Churchill, with a friend saying, "Winston is a man of simple tastes. He is always prepared to put up with the best of everything."

There's a nice touch of humility embedded in both of those phrasings: While Wilde and Churchill are clearly asking for the top drawer and the fine china, they're also suggesting that the best in any category is perfectly acceptable to them. It's spoken like an omnivore, and with enough humor to defuse any anxiety on the part of the host. It's worth comparing this to the phrase "Only the best will do," used the world over as a tagline for premium brands. There's a psychological term for those who go through life demanding only the best: "maximizer." These people, as Barry Schwartz describes in his book *The Paradox of Choice*, are invariably unhappy. How do you pick a restaurant, a pair of jeans, a career, or a spouse if only the best will do? You look for the best option available at the time and then dedicate the rest of your life to calibrating regret based on what's since come on the market. It's a horrible way to live.

Even if you aren't going to be an absolutist about quality, "only the best" is a facetious way to describe your preferences, one used by omnivores the world over to short-circuit any discussion of taste. In this usage, everyone agrees on what quality is, and thus you can serve Oscar a hamburger, pad thai, waffles, beans on toast, or lobster bisque and he wouldn't object. But in reality quality is as ineffable as taste, and to use one as an answer to the other is like answering a question with a question. What do you like? Good stuff. Well, *thanks.* That hardly makes choosing which movie to watch tonight easier, unless we sort all the options by star rating and simply pick the top entry. (Which is still just an average of subjective opinions.) And if we were to attend a concert and you said you'd see anything that sounded good, would we see the historically accurate baroque ensemble or the pitch-perfect Oasis cover band?

And yet, there's nothing wrong with eliminating the shoddy, the half-baked, and the ill-formed from contention before making your selection. If you don't wear fast-fashion clothing because you insist on high-quality stitching, great. If you skip movies starring a certain actress because her stilted delivery ruins every scene she's in, terrific. And if you avoid hot dogs because you've seen how the sausage gets made, bon appétit. You have applied a very useful filter in the process of determining what you like—but it's only one filter, and the results are still so vast as to be unhelpful to anyone trying to buy you a birthday present.

Which brings us to luxurious bitterness. One of the signs of a luxury item is the time and work that went into crafting it—and as we have seen, it takes time and work to appreciate the bitter. Because it's not popular, the bitter will always be in short supply. And it will probably cost you. But if you go for bitter, you are avoiding false distinctions and unctuous upselling. As a discerning consumer, you are putting the emphasis on your discernment instead of your consumption. If only the best will do, it's better to go bitter.

TASTING NOTE: FUTURIST COOKING

Sweet: 10 percent

Sour: 0 percent

Salty: 0 percent

Bitter: 70 percent

Umami: 20 percent

The Futurist Cookbook, an art prank first published in 1932 by Italian poet Filippo Tomasso Marinetti, pretends to be about food but is actually about all of life—so in a sense it's a model for this book. The poor saps who tried to make a meal from Marinetti's manifesto would have to throw out their cutlery, deploy electric fans to waft perfumes at the table, stuff their chickens with ball bearings, deep-fry rose petals, and soak their salamis in espresso. Actual nutrition was off the menu; Marinetti proposed that vitamin pills would take care of that. His concern was a zany new recipe for daily life. Futurist cuisine was an entirely impractical artistic statement, though its strenuous opposition to pasta in all its forms would give it some credence with today's low-carb dieters.

Mr. Difficult

No one man in American culture has had as much trouble with the bittersweet as Jonathan Franzen. He writes big, serious books with big, serious aspirations. They often contain difficult characters, difficult scenarios, and difficult outcomes. At the same time, he writes novels about families and relationships, the stuff of sweetness. The families are deeply dysfunctional, in the modern style. And he's not above having a character shoplift a filet of salmon in his pants.

Franzen's position on the border of bitter and sweet is what set him up for his famous falling-out with Oprah Winfrey in 2001, when the talk-show host chose *The Corrections* for her book club and the author expressed some discomfort at the selection. Specifically, he worried that the Oprah stamp of approval might scare away male readers. Bitter and sweet could mix in his books, but in promotion it just didn't work. The same novel was later to be turned into a premium-cable series, but that project was eventually tabled. The network's explanation captured the same difficulty of mixing the bitter with the sweet, according to a report in *Deadline Hollywood*: "Word is HBO brass liked the performances but the decision came down to adapting the book's challenging narrative, which moves through time and cuts forward and back. While that works in the novel, it proved difficult to sustain in a series and challenging for viewers to follow, hampering the potential show's accessibility." The repetition of the word "challenging" is a reminder that bitter always trumps sweet when Franzen is involved.

More than any of his actual novels, this is his persona. "Mr. Difficult" was the name of a famous essay he wrote to describe the impossibility of reading the novels of William Gaddis, but then the title seemed to stick to him. He explains how a reader of *The Corrections* wrote him a scathing letter, asking, "Who is it that you are writing for? It surely could not be the average person who just enjoys a good read." In considering his response, he was divided between the instincts of his father, "who admired scholars for their intellect and their large vocabularies and was something of a scholar himself," and those of his mother, "a lifelong anti-elitist who used to get good rhetorical mileage out of the mythical 'average person.'"

In our language, he was (and is) divided between the bitter and the sweet. And that's why he maintains his unique position in pop culture today. There are plenty of serious, dense, and demanding writers who make no effort to appeal to the masses, like Roberto Bolaño, whose magnum opus, *2666*, is a nine-hundred-page novel that describes in detail the rape and murder of more than three hundred Mexican prostitutes. And there are accomplished novelists like Michael Chabon who are deeply influenced by popular culture and adored because of it.

But to both engage with the public *and* almost always reject what is popular, albeit with perpetual discomfort: If it weren't so obviously torturous, it might look like a clever strategy to both stay in the public eye and generate plenty of material in the process.

There's a passage in *The Corrections* in which aspiring screenwriter Chip Lambert explains how he puts a "hump" at the beginning of his screenplay: a dense and difficult section that, if the reader can make it through alive, will be followed by all sorts of narrative rewards. Not surprisingly, many reviewers saw exactly this structure at play in *The Corrections*. Is it a traditional family saga marred by a challenging structure, or is it a series of challenging ideas presented in a traditional way? Is it bitter sweetness or sweet bitterness? *Purity*, his 2015 novel, sharply divided critics along this axis. Writing in the *Atlantic*, Caleb Crain said Franzen's sentences had grown "silly and slack," but that this was perhaps evidence of the author's attempt to "eavesdrop more closely on characters." Maybe sweetness was bitterness in disguise? That novel is also headed for a premium-cable adaptation—yet another sign that we love to walk the sweet-bitter divide, and that as long as we do, Mr. Difficult's struggle will continue.

Bitter Art

If the defining taste of high culture is bitter, and the defining characteristic of bitterness is that it is hard to like, what happens when high culture is easy to like?

The art world is constantly confronting this question, though not in these terms. This debate is much more likely to use language we have already deemed useless: good taste and bad taste.

"There is nothing worse than good taste," Jonathan Jones wrote in the *Guardian* in 2010. "And there is nothing more absurd than someone who aspires to show good taste in contemporary art."

"Bad taste often passes for avant-garde taste these days—so long as the artist signals 'transgressive' intent," replied Richard B.

Woodward in *ARTnews*. "And whereas kitsch in art was once to be assiduously disdained, art that traffics in sentimentality and bathos behind a dancing veil of ironic laughter has become highly prized."

The whole merry-go-round is encapsulated in that back-and-forth, such that it's not even necessary to identify the works that got everyone excited in the first place. It's enough to see the broad strokes: Art deliberately provokes until the audience becomes numb, at which point the only way to get a reaction is by shocking them with some conventional beauty. And once that apple cart gains a critical mass of massed critics, it's time to flip it over and start again. It has to stay bitter.

There may be no clearer example of the art-world instinct toward contrarianism than Studio Job. The Belgian design duo is vocally and resolutely opposed to all things smooth, minimal, and sleek. If it features clean lines and an unobtrusive appearance, they hate it.

Which means that they basically hate everything about our modern world. Because the combination of globalization, Instagram, cosmopolitanism, and Pinterest has created an aesthetic so universal, you probably don't even notice it. The cultural critic Kyle Chayka calls this AirSpace, after the phenomenon of so many hosts on the Airbnb home-rental network decorating their residences to the same "neutered Scandinavianism of HGTV." Chayka describes AirSpace as follows:

> It's the realm of coffee shops, bars, start-up offices, and co-live/work spaces that share the same hallmarks everywhere you go: a profusion of symbols of comfort and quality, at least to a certain connoisseurial mind-set. Minimalist furniture. Craft beer and

avocado toast. Reclaimed wood. Industrial lighting. Cortados.
Fast Internet. The homogeneity of these spaces means that trav-
eling between them is frictionless . . . Changing places can be as
painless as reloading a website.

It's the self-declared job of artists like Studio Job to add some
friction to that traveling. They do so by flipping the script, defining
that unobtrusively stylish AirSpace aesthetic with exactly the word
that would traditionally define what they do: "kitsch." The German
term directly translates as "gaudy" and "trashy," and generally means
the complete opposite of neutered Scandinavianism.

"We all live surrounded by kitsch," Job Smeets of Studio Job
told the *New York Times*, "and with things that we assume are good
taste but are bad taste—and the other way around."

Which is how Studio Job explains *Burj Khalifa*, their twelve-
foot-tall 2014 sculpture that depicts King Kong climbing to the top
of the titular Emirati skyscraper. The ape is being buzzed by bi-
planes with working propellers and Islamic symbols, while the base
of the sculpture includes a re-creation of Al-Khazneh temple in
Petra, Jordan, as well as a working clock. The whole piece is covered
in bronze, silver, gold, and Swarovski crystals. It is part of the
Landmark series, which also includes an upside-down Taj Mahal
coffee table and a relatively restrained Eiffel Tower gooseneck lamp.
None of it would work in your living room, which is why their 2016
New York retrospective was arranged as though it were someone's
living room. The curator of that show told the writer Blake Gopnik
he almost coined a new term to describe the duo's work: "metapost-
modernism."

In a later piece for artnet news, Gopnik explains the point of

Studio Job's work, beyond just trolling critics by saying that day is night: "Studio Job is at last helping design catch up with fine art, where for many decades now the most important pieces have been totally unsuited to home use. Who can imagine having an Anri Sala video projection or Jeff Koons porn painting over the sofa? And yet a certain aggressive tastefulness is still the main criterion for 'good' design, as it has almost always been."

If you make a garish painting, no one will bat an eye; it fits into a long line of garish paintings. The same goes for sculpture. But if you say it's a piece of design, or in other words a prototype of a work meant for the masses, well, then people may begin to quibble about where exactly the twelve-foot-high Dubai skyscraper will go in their rec room. (You may have to squeeze it in sideways.)

In other words, if you want to challenge convention, it's much better to be a designer than an artist. "Because if Tynagel and Smeets simply got counted as 'artists,'" Gopnik writes, "their works would then have to be 'sculptures,' and not much more extreme, even in their bad taste, than many others that are out there in the art world."

The lesson here is that it's all but impossible to pucker the mouths of those who spend all their lives consuming bitter things. You build up a resistance. But a touch of bitterness on the plate of someone who isn't used to it goes a long, long way. Serving a quadruple-hopped IPA to a beer snob is like showing a jewel-encrusted table to a collector of modern art: don't expect more than a slightly raised eyebrow. But put that beer into the glass of a lager lover, or that table under the industrial lighting of an Airbnb host, and you're much more likely to get a reaction.

Palate Cleanser

The Myth of Supertasters

A rthur L. Fox owed his success as a chemist to his sloppiness. That sounds like a harsh judgment, but he admitted as much in front of his distinguished colleagues.

"Some time ago the author had occasion to prepare a quantity of phenyl-thio-carbamide and while placing it in a bottle the dust flew around in the air," Fox told the National Academy of Sciences in 1931. "Another occupant of the laboratory, Dr. C. R. Noller, complained of the bitter taste of the dust, but the author, who was much closer, observed no taste and so stated. He even tasted some of the crystals and assured Dr. Noller they were tasteless but Dr. Noller was equally certain it was the dust he tasted."

History does not record all the chemists who accidentally ingested bitter lab dust and didn't live to tell the tale, let alone those scientists who exposed their lab partners to mysterious substances. Happily, Fox's accident was not only harmless but revelatory: this dust, known as PTC, tastes extremely bitter to some people, but has no taste to others. Fox couldn't figure this out: he taste-tested the compound with different ages, sexes, and ethnicities and found a seemingly random distribution of what he termed tasters and nontasters.

Soon after, the American geneticist Albert Blakeslee deduced that "inability to taste the crystals appears to be inherited as a Mendelian recessive." Like attached earlobes and a cleft chin, there are just some people who can taste the powder and some who cannot. Poetically, Blakeslee wrote that "Evidence is thus given for the belief that humans are born with innate differences in respect to all their senses and that different people live in different worlds, therefore, so far as their sensory reactions are concerned."

More than sixty years later, Linda Bartoshuk inadvertently brought the study of PTC (and its safer cousin, 6-n-propylthiouracil, or PROP) into the public imagination. First, Dr. Bartoshuk used statistical analyses to see what Dr. Fox couldn't: that women were much more likely to taste something bitter. She also tested these subjects' reactions to a wide range of other foods, from cheddar cheese to chili peppers. And she devised a new way to rate taste intensity, asking her guinea pigs to tell her how loud the taste would be if it were a sound. (That made more sense to her than having them taste, say, a saltwater control solution.)

This led her to another discovery, one best explained with a bit of high school genetics. To simplify somewhat, your inability to taste PTC's bitterness is a recessive trait, meaning both your mother and your father need to pass it down to you. We can write this as "bb," and this condition describes Dr. Fox. If your mother passes down a dominant gene and your father gives you the recessive gene, you end up as Bb and you can taste the bitterness. (Or vice versa for bB, with the same effect.) What Dr. Bartoshuk investigated was what happened to people who had dominant genes from both parents, or BB. Were these people extrasensitive to bitterness?

Indeed, she found that this group "perceived greater sweetness from sugars but not from aspartame, greater bitterness from several bitter compounds, greater bitterness and irritation from ethyl alcohol, and greater oral burn from capsaicin." She called them supertasters, a name that immediately became a media sensation. She also used a simple physical test to sort her tasters: by staining their tongues with blue dye, she observed more taste receptors on supertasters than on regular tasters or nontasters.

"For about a quarter of the population, sugar may taste sweeter and hot peppers burn hotter than for the rest of us," the Associated Press reported in 1991. "New research suggests that these 'supertasters' can thank their genes and maybe even an unusual abundance of taste buds."

This was where the hype machine began. Restaurant and wine critics, eager to appear genetically predisposed to their occupations, proclaimed themselves supertasters. New diets were concocted for the different groups. And diners looking for a trendy excuse to avoid their broccoli could now blame their genes.

As Linda Bartoshuk and others have noted, the science often got lost in the excitement. Most commonly, the PROP test for bitterness was conflated with the taste bud count, so as soon as someone tasted bitterness they put on their supertaster capes—though, of course, that just meant they were in the 75 percent of the population without the recessive gene for one specific chemical. "Initially, lots of people accepted that definition," she told *Science* in 2010. "I think we were sloppy about it." And, she continued, the very term "super-taster" oversells the phenomenon. "It's not actually true that their taste is super," she said. "It's just different."

And a 2011 review of all the science since Bartoshuk first coined the term could best be described as "exasperated." The authors point out that PROP alone is meaningless, that the word "supertaster" is inaccurate, and that the confusion in the popular imagination is probably beyond repair. Their solution: replace the word "super-taster" with "hypergueisa," from the Greek for overtaste. They're just the people who taste too much, those with "broad, elevated chemo-sensory response across stimuli." Let the public have their super-tasters, along with their brontosauruses, the planet Pluto, and other ideas science has long abandoned; the real scientists will now be talking about hyperguesia.

So where does that leave us, in our markedly nonscientific cam-paign to connect gustatory and aesthetic tastes? Consider what Arthur Fox first noticed: there are certain substances that seem ap-pallingly bitter to some people but totally benign to others. We all have different internal barometers for our preferences, and just as some foods manage to cleanly divide the population, so too might some works of art. Take the movie *Love Actually* (please!). There is a broad-based affection for the 2003 film that has made it a modern-day holiday classic. There's also a deep strain of hatred for the same movie. For some, it's a gentle tale of how love makes people ridic-ulous and sometimes you just need to give in and tell the world how you feel. This group may adore it, like it, or simply have seen it once and mildly enjoyed it. For others, it's a saccharine, manipulative, regressive, and hateful screed. These are the *Love Actually* supertasters, and even the fact that it stars Alan Rickman can't convince them to watch it again. It's like cinematic cilantro.

The real takeaway is that we all have different senses of taste, both physical and cultural. What is objectively bitter can be intolerable to some and mild to others. A lifetime of sugar can lead some to find the slightest bit cloying and most food sickeningly sweet. Your palate, both physical and cultural, is uniquely your own.

Your palate, both physical and cultural, is uniquely your own.

6

Umami: The Indescribable Taste

Featuring: MORE NORWEGIANS THAN YOU MIGHT EXPECT;
PLUS, MEN WITH HOBBIES

Umami has been called the fifth taste, and it's commonly said to have been discovered just over a century ago. When strung together like that, those two facts seem astounding. It sounds as though we're saying there was an eighth color in the rainbow and it was only noticed this year, or that there was a fifth Beatle all along and we never saw him because he always stood directly behind Ringo.

But that assumes that the four tastes are some sort of Newtonian law handed down by evolution, when they are in fact a basic consensus. You were likely taught that sweet, sour, salty, and bitter are the basic tastes, just as there are three primary colors and five senses. These nice round numbers sound like science, but the formal criteria for a basic taste—those with specific chemical receptors on the tongue—are relatively new. Humans muddled through for centuries with a rough compromise. Aristotle identified the basic four along with astringent, pungent, and harsh. Jean Fernel added fattiness in 1542, and to that the Swedish botanist Carolus Linnaeus added sharp, viscous, insipid, aqueous, and nauseous. The Swiss anatomist Albrecht von Haller threw in rough, urinous, spiritous, aromatic, acrid, and putrid. In 1825, our man Jean-Anthelme Brillat-Savarin cleared the decks with his statement that "the number of tastes is infinite, since every soluble body has a special flavor which does not wholly resemble any other." But if infinity seems a bit much, he's willing to narrow it down to two: agreeable and disagreeable.

So when Japanese scientist Kikunae Ikeda proposed the taste of umami in 1908, it wasn't quite like the discovery of a new planet. Everyone knew the basic four didn't truly cover everything we put in our mouths, but it was hard to agree on what further categories made sense. Somehow, though, umami clicked in a way that the more direct fattiness did not (but give it time: the campaign to classify fat as the sixth taste may well be successful in the near future). It identified a glutinous taste, one common in the seaweed-friendly Japanese diet but also found in foods like tomatoes, fish, meat, and cheese. It's similar to salty but not quite the same, and is described as meaty but is present in many vegetables. Ikeda had synthesized glutamate from the kombu seaweed, and he could add it to other foods to give them an umami taste.

He presented this finding to the Eighth International Congress of Applied Chemistry in Washington and New York in 1912, where he referenced the big four tastes and went on to note that there was something similar in the tastes of asparagus, cheese, tomatoes, and meat that couldn't be explained by the other tastes. That something was glutamate.

The funny thing is that glutamate on its own had no real flavor.

A spoonful of salt mixed into a glass of water will taste salty. A spoonful of glutamate mixed in water will taste like nothing much. It boosts its companions as the wingman of flavors.

Ikeda resigned from his post at the University of Tokyo before retirement age, and in explaining why, he was openly dismissive of his extremely lucrative discovery. Umami made money—an embarrassing amount of it—in the form of Ajinomoto, the first commercially available monosodium glutamate. Previously, the Japanese had to boil down kelp to get glutamate. By combining it with sodium, it could now be sold as soup stock, and within a decade it was available around the world.

The meaning of umami, for our purposes, is that taste that we clearly crave but can't quite identify. The sweetness of sugar is an obvious draw, and scarfing a bag of gummy bears at your desk at around four p.m. on a Tuesday has a noticeable and desirable effect, at least until you crash at four forty-five. But why you might want the umaminess of a tomato is subtler and a harder thing to put into words. We still eat plenty of tomatoes, even if we don't speak of having an umami tooth or getting an umami high. It's too subtle for that. Preferences that scratch an itch we can't easily identify are umami.

> *Preferences that scratch an itch we can't easily identify are umami.*

When we map it onto cultural taste, it's similarly hard to pin down. The fifth entertainment preference was cerebral, or essentially straight-up information: documentaries, reference books, home-improvement shows, and financial news, all filled with facts and aimed at audiences described as older, self-assured, enterprising, and curious. It's something consumed because it feels necessary, and that's that. It's food for thought: not something you would usually choose to binge on, and something traditionally considered highbrow. So when we talk about umami culture, we'll talk about the self-awareness that comes with it. In food, unless you follow culinary culture, it's quite easy to be unaware of umami in a way that you can't be unaware of the sweet, sour, salty, and bitter. But once you know it, you taste it everywhere and seek it out. A broader definition of umami will extend this effect: umami culture is about a taste that is so necessary it can taste like nothing at all, a miso broth that satisfies without explanation. How do they do that, anyway?

Oddly Satisfying Norwegians, Part I: Karl Ove Knausgaard

The novels of Karl Ove Knausgaard are the pinnacle of umami culture. The six-volume series, *My Struggle*, which describes the Norwegian's life in copious, exacting, and mind-numbing detail, is nearly devoid of what is conventionally called a plot. The sentences are clunky and full of clichés. The effect of the books is almost impossible to replicate in small doses—you need to let them wash over you, page after page describing how he took his daughter to a birthday party. (A gathering that clocks in at fifty pages.) But they've been phenomenally successful, among no group more so than the literati.

Why? In *The Chronicle of Higher Education*, Tom Bartlett made fun of how professional readers constantly "attempt, usually with much sputtering and little success, to explain their bent-knee devotion. See, it's a plotless novel focused on the excruciatingly mundane life of a hypersensitive guy in Norway"—and then they lose the listener.

Ben Lerner put it best in his review of volume three in the *London Review of Books*: "It's easy to marshal examples of what makes *My Struggle* mediocre. The problem is: it's amazing." He alludes to the frequent use of drug metaphors to describe the books' appeal, and cites the literary critic Michael Clune's observation that the drug metaphor is used when "we find ourselves taking pleasure in a book without being able to ascribe our interest to respectable literary values." Or to put it another way, when we like something without really knowing why.

The literary world is a good place to look for these kinds of unidentifiable itches, probably because only a great facility with language can allow you to come close to describing something so slippery. Lydia Davis, the great American short story writer, did this when she explained her work as a translator in a column for the *Times Literary Supplement*.

"In spite of having translated during most of my life, I still don't really understand the urge," she wrote. "Why can't I simply enjoy reading the story in its own language. Or, on the other hand, why can't I be content to write my own work in English? The urge is a kind of hunger; maybe the polite word would be appetite—I want to consume the text, and reproduce it in English."

She considers the obvious explanation, that perhaps translation gives her the satisfaction of having written without the need to actually write, the "pleasure of composing it in English, without the uncertainty involved in inventing it." All the taste, half the calories. And there's also the feeling of "acquisitiveness," of taking something that isn't hers. Ultimately, though, she concludes that the "desire to translate may be something of an inexplicable addiction."

Outside the rarefied air of the literary world, there is a large subset of people who derive these sorts of hard-to-describe pleasurable sensations from unexpected sources. We can call what these individuals are experiencing "umami culture" precisely because they don't know what to call it themselves. It's not so much a situation where the glass is half-full as a situation in which you know the glass is full to the brim of something you enjoy but you have no idea what that mysterious drink is.

Naturally, these people have set up a subreddit. The Web forum called Oddly Satisfying, and it's described as a place "you can post things that make you feel, well, oddly satisfied. This can be physical (like popping bubble wrap), visual (a perfectly looped GIF), or even aural (the crunching of leaves)."

The bubble-wrap example has been studied by psychologists, or at least one psychologist. In her 1992 paper "Popping Sealed Air Capsules to Reduce Stress," Kathleen Dillon describes how a group of students reported increased levels of both calm and alertness after being granted access to bubble wrap. She links the poppable plastic bubbles to Catholic rosary beads and what antiquarians call "fingering pieces": carved bits of jade carried for, well, fingering. Dillon and the very few subsequent investigators of this topic never quite get to a satisfying explanation of why it's satisfying. As she told the

New York Times, "It's obviously something that's desirable and addictive at some level."

The visual equivalent is best represented by GIFs of perfectly rendered industrial processes. In a video compilation of these animations posted to YouTube, viewers expressed satisfaction (often in sexual terms, and in language you might expect if you have ever read comments on YouTube) as well as confusion about the source of that satisfaction.

"Have you ever seen something that makes your skin tingle and for some unknown reason provides you with a sense of unbridled peace and happiness? Gears working in perfect synchronization, a cake frosted with absolute precision, marbles rolling so smoothly it hurts. Something that is just . . . satisfying?" reads the description of this video posted by Digg. "Well, here's five solid minutes of that feeling."

As one commenter wrote, "Retitle this: Interesting technical and mechanical feats." Another wrote "How to get high w/o drugs for free." Many mentioned obsessive-compulsive disorder, and a few referenced ASMR, or autonomous sensory meridian response, a low-grade euphoria caused by whisper-like sounds and described by *Vice* as "the good feeling no one can explain." It is, despite its clinical-sounding name, almost entirely ignored by science, though it's very popular on the Internet. It is, as many (but not all) of its proponents stress, not at all sexual, but rather a tingling feeling that resembles being scratched on the head from the inside. Beyond whispers and the crinkling of candy wrappers, other commonly mentioned triggers include watching people in deep concentration, seeing people borrow your belongings, or getting the sort of personal attention required for a haircut or massage.

It is similar but not identical to a flow state, the phenomenon of being totally immersed in what you're doing and, according to Mihaly Csikszentmihalyi, the researcher who developed the idea, the "psychology of optimal experience."

If watching a tomato being sliced to perfection, hearing someone whisper instructions in Spanish, and popping bubble wrap elicit reactions like those that so many people have described in their responses to reading the life story of Karl Ove Knausgaard, do the activities share some fundamental property?

Arguably, it is this: they're all about getting the details fully and completely right, no matter how dull, repetitive, or pointless that seems. It's what psychologists call the "completion principle," our natural desire to see all loops closed so we can admire the symmetry of the resulting circles. Plenty of people won't see the point in that, and that's fine for them. For those who give it time, there's an odd satisfaction to be had.

For Knausgaard, the key is the endless stream of details, all washing over the reader until you are fully immersed. As reader Douglas Feil explained on Goodreads, there are three possible explanations of Knausgaard's methodology:

- "He knew he was going to write this novel from a very early age and therefore set about remembering and notating every single detail of his life, mundane or not. Genius.
- "His memory failed him and he couldn't remember anything, except for the major incidences, and therefore was forced to make up all the details, and every single minor observation is fiction. Genius.

- "It's a combination of both. He remembered some things, and what he didn't, he had to relive or re-observe. He literally went back to his grandmother's home and cleaned the railing with a rag and detergent and then recorded his observations as they would've occurred had he remembered every detail. Genius!"

No matter where these details came from, the attention to them is amazing. And not just the interesting ones, but all of them! In that way, it fills in the huge gaps between everything else. Almost every other book, film, or TV show is about (or at least aspires to be about) interesting stuff happening. But the underwhelming majority of our lives are not about interesting stuff happening (that's why we need these books/movies/TV shows to consume when we're on the plane, waiting for a bus, or idly sitting at home). Knausgaard completes the story by telling us the boring bits, what one critic termed "the dense material accumulations that make up our lives, and which are essentially trivial"—and that's oddly satisfying. Indeed, everything that falls under the category "oddly satisfying" also fits as "essentially trivial."

Many of his most ardent fans report that they mix up his memories with theirs, combining their biographies. It's a form of total artistic immersion.

TASTING NOTE: MASSIVELY MULTIPLAYER
ONLINE ROLE-PLAYING GAMES

Sweet: 20 percent
Sour: 20 percent
Salty: 0 percent
Bitter: 0 percent
Umami: 60 percent

The 2016 novel *The Nix* follows a frustrated English professor who is addicted to an online multiplayer fantasy game. He locks the door to his office, turns off the lights, and spends endless hours plotting to slay dragons with his elven peers. Why? The clinical data on what's been called Internet Gaming Disorder is inconclusive, but there is certainly something addictive about understanding and conquering a meticulously created universe. As author Nathan Hill explains it, "these quests—which usually involved slaying some minor enemy or delivering a message across treacherous terrain or locating some lost important doodad—needed to be completed without fail for up to forty days in a row to unlock rewards in the *fastest time mathematically possible*, which itself was a kind of reward because whenever he was successful at it these fireworks went off and there was this blast of trumpets and he got his name on the public chart of *Elfscape*'s Most Epic Players and everyone on his contact list sent him notes of congratulation and praise." It's worth noting that Slack, the wildly popular intra-office chat tool, was the fallback project of a company that was trying to build a similar MMORPG. After all, isn't all of office life just another role-playing game full of quests and rewards?

Oddly Satisfying Norwegians, Part II: Slow TV

There's another possible explanation for Karl Ove, one that emerges when we look to the country that created him. Is there something in the Norwegian water? If so, it might explain the Slow TV phenomenon, which is essentially the AV extension of Knausgaard's books. Slow TV is a series that premiered on Norway's state broadcaster in 2009 with a single-camera episode of the seven-hour train ride from Bergen to Oslo. It attracted a huge audience, and subsequent installments included:

- 134 hours of a cruise ship sailing along the coastline (watched at least in part by 3.2 million viewers)
- 18 hours of salmon fishing—and they didn't catch anything until hour three (1.6 million viewers)
- 13 hours of knitting ("From Sheep to Sweater," 1 million viewers)

Are Norwegians nuts? "I don't think we are," Slow TV creator Thomas Hellum said in an interview with the TED Radio Hour.

"I think we have, with the slow TV, we have done something that reacts to a need among people. Trying to tell a story in full length, it can be a window to the world. And if you go on a train journey, if you go on a boat journey, you experience in the same slow way. And that's made me appreciate slowness because it gives the viewer a possibility to take back some of the control."

It isn't just a Norwegian phenomenon either. In August 2016, more than a million Britons tuned in to BBC4's *The Country Bus* to watch a bus driving around the Yorkshire countryside. In the same year, the Icelandic band Sigur Ros debuted *Route One* on their nation's television and YouTube, taking viewers on a twenty-four-hour drive along the island nation's ring road. (Arguably, Andy Warhol invented the whole genre with *Sleep*, his 1963 film of the poet John Giorno slumbering for five hours and twenty minutes.)

The similarities between Knausgaard and Slow TV have been debated and disputed. The critic Nathan Heller noted that the key difference is that the books are "filtered, varied, and enlivened" by the author's point of view, while the videos are "unshaped by interior consciousness." But their innate umaminess is much bigger than that. It's about a nearly endless stream of information, and our similarly sized appetite for that information.

TASTING NOTE: JOHN HODGMAN

Sweet: 10 percent
Sour: 0 percent
Salty: 5 percent
Bitter: 20 percent
Umami: 65 percent

John Hodgman's rise to fame began with a fanciful list of hobo names. There are seven hundred of them in *The Areas of My Expertise*, the former literary agent's 2005 fake almanac, and this list led to a recurring gig as *The Daily Show*'s resident expert, two sequel almanacs, and a collaborative Internet project to illustrate each of these "broken souls who had taken to the wandering life." The list is as deeply umami as Hodgman's persona as a whole: so full of facts that the fact the facts are fictions only makes them more savory.

Martin Parr and the Mundane

At the time of this book's publication, it was still possible to purchase postcards at tourist destinations around the world. Most of these postcard vendors will even sell you stamps, with which you can send these impersonal if professional photographs across weeks and through multiple postal services to friends and relatives. The whole process is riddled with more anachronisms than any other in everyday life, save perhaps buying a newspaper.

In the pockets of most tourists—assuming tourism requires a certain level of affluence—is a smartphone that can (a) take photos that are as good or better than those on the postcard, in sheer image quality but especially in relevance to what the traveler has actually seen, (b) send these photos to the aforementioned friends and relatives seconds after taking them, or (c) post those photos to Instagram and ensure that the photographer's entire social network wishes they were there.

The degree to which this improves on a postcard is an order of magnitude beyond how, say, an e-book improves on a book. And yet we still have postcards.

What pictures do we put on these ancient modes of communication? The salty seaside cartoons discussed earlier are relics now, leaving behind a pretty but bland collection of landmarks, sunsets, and points of interest. There are postcards of St. Peter's Square and the Eiffel Tower and Mount Everest—but there are also postcards of the Holiday Inn Hotel of Huntsville, Alabama, and the Unicentre and Bus Station in Preston, UK.

It is these postcards—the minor landmarks—that have been brought to prominence by the British photographer Martin Parr. In his books *Boring Postcards* and *Boring Postcards USA*, he doesn't really live down to his titles, and he's admitted as much.

"I think they're absolutely interesting—the title is a way to get people's attention," he told an interviewer. "In fact they have this whole layer of information and revelation about the society behind them."

These well-photographed office parks, motels, highway overpasses, and shopping plazas are fascinating specimens of a long-gone era. There are examples of midcentury modern architecture, neatly made hotel beds, bowls of truck-stop chili, and aluminum awnings. Nearly all of them shine with civic pride—why, yes, Dayton has a municipal airport, and thanks for noticing!

To send this to a loved one is contrived perfectionism of the everyday; it's the 1950s version of Beyoncé's boast that she woke up like this.

It's also proof that few things are truly boring, and if something is widely deemed boring it's almost certainly not. There are hundreds of postcards of the Statue of Liberty, but the Dayton Airport likely has only a few. The fact that there probably hasn't been a Dayton Airport postcard made since, and never will be again, is interesting in its own way.

Especially when you look at postcards like this next to the photos that made Martin Parr famous in the first place: regular people on holiday.

His Small World collection documents the people taking pictures of the places: The three tourists each pretending as though they're holding up the Leaning Tower of Pisa for their own photographer, for instance. The crowd in front of the Acropolis, posing with their backs to yet another crowd. The man in shorts, on horseback, eyes pressed on a large camcorder.

Is Parr being mean to these vacationers? In his introduction to one of the Small World books, Geoff Dyer says, well, maybe but instantly forgives him: "[T]he people in these photographs would recognize themselves and their fellow travelers. They would agree that, although they have chosen and paid to come to these places, sightseeing in particular and holidaying generally are often the opposite of fun—partly because of all the other tourists." These people are fools and they are us.

> *These people are fools and they are us.*

So no matter how you holiday, Martin Parr has your number. His work falls squarely into umami culture because it is a flavor we would miss without him. Had he not collected these postcards or framed these tourists, we would have looked right past them. (As we inevitably do when we are sightseeing.) He's not exactly addictive or oddly satisfying on a Norwegian scale; instead, he is a background flavor that's been there all along. To notice it, and to think about what it means, is a deeply umami experience.

The actual umami taste is the taste of decay. The glutamate in broth is released by boiling bones, kelp, or whatever other protein source you are using, denaturing the proteins within and releasing the amino acid that tastes like umami. So it's fitting that Martin Parr has made the gradual unraveling of things his central obsession.

"Decline is so much more interesting than success," he told the *Financial Times*. "And decline photographs very well. We are surrounded by propaganda, interviews with glamorous people and so on. They have their own agenda. Decline, or something going downhill, is automatically more interesting to me."

There was a time when postcards were the fastest way to communicate, back in the Edwardian era when the mail came seven times a day. That time has passed, and yet postcards linger on, artifacts of decline that are themselves in decline.

And Parr's take on the selfie stick, that modern symptom of decline? It makes his job—photographing the photographers—even easier.

"I welcome this trend as, interestingly, you can get the whole scene in front of the camera and the backdrop all in one photo," he wrote on his blog. "Previously I had to make do with photos of people from behind as they looked at the view."

Decline is everywhere, and it can be delicious.

TASTING NOTE: *GILMORE GIRLS*

Sweet: 40 percent
Sour: 0 percent
Salty: 0 percent
Bitter: 20 percent
Umami: 40 percent

The story of a single mother raising her precocious daughter in a New England town filled with lovable oddballs sounds as sweet as a bag of jelly beans. But *Gilmore Girls*, in both its original network run and its Netflix resurrection, has always distinguished itself with a thick layer of cultural references. The show is practically hyperlinked with allusions. And in addition to that information overload, there's that ineffable feeling of satisfaction. The critic Haley Mlotek has called the show "emotionally speculative fiction," a genre that "takes everything recognizable about life but adds the qualities that remain elusively out of reach in reality, like satisfying endings and triumphant character arcs." And that's the rare balance of sweetness and umami.

The Interesting Secret of the Dull Men's Club

If taste is about making a conscious choice to like something, there is a philosophical parse that must be examined: What's more important, the choice or the something? We have posited that no matter what you choose—be it French poodles or Jell-O shots or Rembrandt paintings—you have displayed taste, so it stands to reason that the exercise of taste lives in the choice you have made.

But what if you choose nothing? It's like asking if zero can be a number, or if your pizza toppings can be extra cheese and tomato sauce. If you claim beige as your favorite color, it still counts as a claim. We saw this in basic/normcore, but the recent vintage of those buzzwords is misleading—the choice of not choosing has always been with us. Which brings us to the Dull Men's Club.

This tongue-in-cheek group of Englishmen and Americans proclaim themselves "dull but not boring," and they explain this distinction by saying, "Dull men accept their dullness. Boring men are dull men who actually believe that they are interesting." In this reading, the difference between dull and boring is whether the man minds his own business or not. A larger distinction could be made that the dull do things the rest of the world considers boring, while the boring do things the rest of the world considers normal.

What are those boring things? The 2015 documentary *Born to be Mild* sums up the activities of the Dull Men's Club in a sprightly fifteen minutes. There is the roundabout aficionado who loves the traffic feature built around a duck pond; the letterbox photographer whose son programmed a GPS device to help his dad find this elusive quarry; and the milk bottle collector who casually mentions that he doesn't actually consume the stuff ("I just don't like milk. It's nothing I would ever drink.").

As Jason Kottke wrote, "I could get into milk bottles and roundabouts. What about the truly dull, who don't collect anything and just watch the news on TV all day?" (Again, those people should more accurately be referred to as boring.)

This is fitting, as the cerebral category of our entertainment preferences was filled nearly to the brim with news and informational programming. The profile for this preference tended to be older, male, self-assured, and enterprising. But those CNN viewers have nothing on the umami of the Dull Men's Club. The organization itself is an attempt to describe the indescribable—the pleasure you can derive from something that doesn't seem that pleasurable.

Which is why the Dull Men's Club is really just an elaborate cover for a disparate group that dares not reveal what its members truly are. The trainspotters and grammar pedants of the DMC have *not* chosen to like nothing; they have chosen some very specific somethings, and they are blunting any possible criticism of their esoteric choices by proclaiming their ordinariness. They are something different and very describable: men with hobbies. But they don't describe themselves that way because, well, no one does. Hobbies are umami: deeply absorbing and satisfying but hard to explain to outsiders. On some level, it's better to call yourself dull than to say you're a hobbyist.

An important side note here: Why, it has been asked, are there no girls allowed in this dull treehouse? The answer from the DMC website's Frequently Asked Questions section is distinctly unsatisfying: "Our view is that women are not dull. Women are exciting. Moreover, we think women would be offended if we said they were dull . . . that it would be politically incorrect to refer to women as being dull."

As one critic asked, "Why not simply 'the Dull Club', which also admits women? What are these men scared of? . . . Do they fear there aren't enough lawns and European train timetables and hedges to go round?"

Though the Dull Men don't admit it, the real reason for their gender segregation is at least in part spousal avoidance. And sometimes, it works too well.

"My ex-wife hated the fact that I was a roundabout spotter, and in the end she left me," Kevin Beresford, president of the Roundabout Appreciation Society, says in the documentary *Born to be Mild*. "But I don't mind, because I can go out now roundabout spotting whenever I want."

A Job You Can't Lose

What is a hobby, and what happened to them? The word itself sounds outdated, and as proof of that, an elegy for the hobby appeared in the *New York Times Magazine* in 1997. There, Randy Cohen laid out a series of criteria that defined a hobby, rightly noting that productive or occasional pastimes like cooking and bowling didn't really count.

A hobby requires "a particular—even disproportionate—intensity of attention," he writes. Photographing every mailbox in the United Kingdom certainly qualifies.

Hobbies will necessitate knowing a great deal of "irredeemably specific information," knowledge the leader of the Dull Men (official title: assistant vice president) ably showcases when he explains why airport baggage carousels always move in a counterclockwise direction. (Because this gives right-handed passengers more leverage when they're picking up their bags.)

The hobby should be "absorbing but not transforming. They fill the mind without altering it," Cohen writes. It should be umami. Or as the Dull Men's Club puts it in their explanation that they are not to be confused with Dullards Anonymous: "Twelve-Step Programs are designed to make people change their behaviors. Dull men don't want to change."

And here is the crux of the hobby, the likely cause of death and a good reason for resurrection: the hobby should "provide a strong counterbalance to work." The Dull Men are largely retired, but those who are not appear to split their waking hours evenly between toil and their chosen hobbies.

It is worth noting that the hobby was at its peak in the United States during the Great Depression. It was precisely when jobs were hardest to come by that there was a public preoccupation with what were described as the jobs you couldn't lose. (It would be equally accurate but not quite as appealing to describe them as jobs no one was paying you to do.)

The scholar Steven M. Gelber is perhaps the leading expert on the American hobby, and he describes them as an oxymoron: productive leisure. They inhabit the gray area between work and sloth, "both an escape from and an escape into work." The hobby movement is closely tied to the industrial revolution, as a way to bridge the new distance between toil and play and a tacit acknowledgment that not all jobs could provide creative satisfaction. Hobby proponents would often quote the old proverb about the devil finding work for idle hands, positioning stamp collecting as a necessary fortification against evil. And in the words of one collector of Abraham Lincoln artifacts: "In the hobby kingdom, every man is his own boss, he can pursue his hobby in any direction he chooses, at as fast or slow a pace as he is disposed to set, without interference from a single soul."

And so the demise of the hobby roughly correlates to the rise of the dream of meaningful work—the idea that you could find not only a paycheck but fulfillment at your job, and that you should do what you love and the money will follow. There's perhaps no clearer summary of this ethos than Steve Jobs's speech to the graduates of Stanford University in 2005.

"Your work is going to fill a large part of your life and the only way to be truly satisfied is to do what you believe is great work," he said. "And the only way to do great work is to love what you do. If you haven't found it yet, keep looking. Don't settle."

And yet, there was only one Steve Jobs, and when he and Steve Wozniak built the Apple computer in his parents' garage, they weren't collecting a paycheck.

The writer Cal Newport calls this the passion trap, and defines it as "The more emphasis you place on the work you love, the more unhappy you become when you don't love every minute of the work you have."

If the way out of this trap is to stop insisting on doing work you love, hobbies can fill the gap. Look at it as layering: Work provides money, camaraderie, and some sense of fulfillment. Hobbies provide a sense of agency and deep immersion in a highly personalized passion project. The two may not merge, and that's a good thing: think of the workaholic who retires into an early grave. If and when you're downsized, outsourced, let go, or otherwise put out of work, there should be a silver lining: more time for the thing you really love. A hobby can provide solace if not sustenance.

In a sense, the hobby has already been reborn as the side hustle. This millennial term for the gig a person works in addition to their day job is a tacit acknowledgment that it's rarely possible to exclusively do what you love. The pessimistic view of this is that there are no good jobs for the current generation; the optimistic take is it's never been easier to sample a wide range of occupations. Unlike a pure hobby, the side hustle is generally done for money, but ideally there's more to it than that.

In the words of advertising copywriter/freelance writer Catherine Baab-Muguira, "The side hustle offers something worth much more than money: a hedge against feeling stuck and dull and cheated by life. This psychological benefit is the real reason for the millennial obsession, I'd argue, and why you might want to consider finding your own side hustle, no matter how old you are."

One benefit of this rebranding of the hobby for the second industrial revolution (or whatever you choose to call our current era) is that it's no longer a gendered term. It's not about avoiding your spouse or any other human; it's about, in Baab-Muguira's words, building a "bridge between crass realities and your compelling inner life." Unlike the dull man's hobby, the side hustle can earnestly call itself compelling.

Randy Cohen lamented that hobbies were dying, to be replaced by television and shopping. He didn't foresee the Internet, which streamed television and accelerated shopping but also let hobbyists and side hustlers from around the world find each other.

Once, as an adolescent with an interest in public transit, I visited a model train store to ask if they sold subway replicas. "You know what I told the last guy who asked that?" the man behind the counter barked. "Line up a bunch of shoe boxes on the floor and tell people those are the aboveground stations."

No boy ever need suffer such humiliation again. Hundreds of model subway cars are available at reasonable rates from re-tailers around the world. (The Berliner U-Bahn looks par-ticularly handsome.) Just think of it: a world of dullness, of productive leisure, of side hustling and all the satisfaction that comes with it, is at our fingertips. The correct re-action to this realization is indescribable.

Palate Cleanser

Aging Tastefully

As we age, our tastes change—or in some cases, stop changing. This phenomenon is most clearly documented in physical taste: Numerous studies have shown age-related declines in the ability to taste sweet, sour, salty, bitter, and umami foods. This research usually involves giving senior citizens samples of increasingly concentrated solutions, with the general finding that the older the taster, the more concentrated the taste required to register. (Adding more flavor often means adding salt or sugar, which does nothing to help hypertension and diabetes.) Taste buds stop regenerating, saliva production decreases, and our sense of smell, which contributes so much of the nuance to the flavors of food, deteriorates. It's been estimated that between 60 and 75 percent of people over the age of seventy have what the literature calls "major olfactory impairments." This loss of the ability to taste, both with the tongue and the nose, begins in middle age.

And here again, we make the jump from taste in food to taste in everything else. If life is a trial-and-error process of figuring out what we like, it starts in earnest once we reach adulthood, takes a decade or two, and then slows down. By the time you're into middle age, you've probably got a pretty good idea of what books you like to read, what movies you'll go see, and what songs you like. You may be less likely to accompany friends who are going to see a band you've never heard of, which means you're less susceptible to peer pressure (or, as your peers might see it, less fun). Our social networks tend to shrink as we age, and with them the possibility of being exposed to new tastes recedes as well.

Some of us are stuck in our ways with Velcro and others with superglue, but by a certain age, we all have our ways.

So how do we age tastefully? For the definitive guide to how tastes change as we age, we can turn to W. H. Auden. The English poet sketches the stages of a reader's life in his essay "Reading." (He also declares, quite usefully, that the best way to know if you can trust a critic is to present him with a questionnaire on what Eden looks like. Auden's paradise features a British climate, chemical factories, and religious processions as a main form of public entertainment, so take that under advisement.)

Auden comes to the subject with a refreshing lack of stuffiness. "As readers, most of us, to some degree, are like those urchins who pencil mustaches on the faces of girls in advertisements," he declares. We have to figure out what the author is trying to say, and in the process we often end up defacing the meaning of the book.

Auden divides the life of a scribbling urchin into three main stages:

Childhood. This is when we read for pleasure, but we have no idea what pleasure is. Ideally, this doesn't stop us.

Adolescence. Now, we want some guidance, and we look for a mentor. We're quite likely to bend our natural preferences into the shape suggested by this elder statesman: The reader "has to pretend that he enjoys olives or *War and Peace* a little more than he actually does."

Early adulthood. Here's where Auden breaks from conventional wisdom: between the ages of twenty and forty, when you'd likely assume all your most sophisticated tastes are formed, we are indeed "engaged in the process of discovering who we are." But this is trickier than we assume, as we must figure out the difference between what we can force ourselves to appreciate and what we're just never going to like. This process, by Auden's watch, takes two decades:

"When someone between twenty and forty says, apropos of a work of art, 'I know what I like,' he is really saying, 'I have no taste of my own but accept the taste of my cultural milieu,' because, between twenty and forty, the surest sign that a man has a genuine taste of his own is that he is uncertain of it."

This is a ringing denouncement of what could arguably be called the prime of life. Certainly the vast majority of artists break through during these years, and Auden was no exception. That said, his early poetry is beautiful but fairly incomprehensible. In the 1960s, at around the same time this analysis of reading life was published, he wrote in the preface to one of his reissued early works that he couldn't "think myself back into the frame of mind in which I wrote it. My name on the title page seems a pseudonym for someone else, someone talented but near the border of sanity, who might well in a year or two become a Nazi." Instead, he figured out who he was: the Auden who wrote "Stop all the clocks," of the "low dishonest decade," and "If equal affection cannot be,/Let the more loving one be me" was the Auden of . . .

Middle age. Here we have our winner. It's no coincidence that this analysis of reading life was published when the poet was in his fifties. The faculties of taste govern both inputs and outputs. The fog of early influence had cleared and he knew what he wanted to write—and presumably also wanted to read. The life of the mind begins at forty. (It should be noted this is by no means a unanimous opinion: the poet may have been happier with his later work, but many critics were not. Philip Larkin wrote dismissively of a "loss of vividness, a tendency to rehearse themes already existing as literature, a certain abstract windiness" in later Auden.)

> *The life of the mind begins at forty.*

Once you've left the others behind, closed the door, and figured out what you really want to read, watch, eat, hear, or do, then you will know your taste. If you've made it all the way over the hill without losing your true self, you can finally read for pleasure again—only now, you'll know what you like. And what you'll like next.

7

Harmony: How to Put It All Together

Featuring: PORK BUNS, BLTS, *HAMILTON*,
CURATORS, DIANA VREELAND, DECORATIVE BRUTALITY,
ALGORITHMS, AND YOU

Now that we have journeyed to the five corners of taste, we come to the center. What does it look like when sweet, sour, salty, bitter, and umami are in perfect balance?

Heinz ketchup, as we learned from Malcolm Gladwell at the very beginning. But now that we've translated the tastes into culture, it deserves a larger answer. How many foods *do* feature the five tastes in perfect harmony? This question is much more integral to Asian cuisine than the Western palate, and it's more likely to operate on the level of a meal than an individual dish. A sour soup is balanced by a sweet stir-fry, which is in turn complemented by a bitter sauce. The Chinese philosopher and chef Yi Yin, who was thinking and cooking around 1600 B.C.E, articulated a theory of five tastes, albeit with pungent instead of umami. He wrote that when the tastes were properly balanced, *the transformation which occurs in the cauldron is quintessential and wondrous, subtle and delicate. The mouth cannot express it in words; the mind cannot fix upon an analogy. It is like the subtlety of archery and horsemanship, the transformation of yin and yang, or the revolution of the four seasons. Thus it is long-lasting yet does not spoil; thoroughly cooked yet not mushy; sweet yet not cloying; sour yet not corrosive; salty yet not deadening; pungent yet not acrid; mild yet not insipid; oily-smooth yet not greasy.*

And keep in mind these are the words of a man who never got to try Heinz ketchup.

From the culinary world, then, we have two ways to think about harmony in taste. You can have it in every mouthful or in every meal. Creating a single dish that hits all the right notes—harmonics on the level of a mouthful—mirrors the thinking of one of the most interesting chefs of our time.

Harmony in the Kitchen: Building a Balanced Dish

This idea of breaking down genres to their components and then re-categorizing them along the lines of the five basic physical tastes—the whole premise of the Elements of Taste—is already being used to great effect in the many kitchens of David Chang.

We know this because the chef behind the Momofuku restaurant empire laid out his Unified Theory of Deliciousness in *WIRED* magazine. The gist of it is that flavor relationships cut across cultures, so that the pleasure you derive from a BLT—the "steamed bread, fatty meat, cool crunch"—is identical to that of the

Momofuku pork bun, even though the cultural history of the two dishes is radically different.

Chang's belief is that the surest path to restaurant success is to play the hits well—to make steak frites that reminds diners of every great steak frites they've ever eaten. But to really blow minds, you need to "evoke those taste memories while cooking something that seems unfamiliar—to hold those base patterns constant while completely changing the context."

The result is a dish that you have a deep emotional connection to even if you have no idea why that is. Chang borrows the term "strange loop" from the cognitive scientist Douglas Hofstadter to describe this sensation, and it can perhaps be simplified as the gustatory equivalent of asking what came first, the chicken or the egg? (Though not by serving a chicken frittata.)

To make these dishes, Chang draws upon the five tastes, substituting, for example, the umami of fermented chickpeas for that of pecorino cheese in the classic pasta dish *cacio e pepe*. And with this formula, he can create culinary hits—dishes that bring new ideas to beloved recipes in order to give people something novel that they've always loved. That is taste harmony, and it works as well in the culture as it does in the kitchen.

A TASTING MENU FOR THE CONNOISSEUR

As per our discussion of bitter luxury, for you, only the best will do. You want to know not only the best, but how to tell the best in class apart from the merely excellent. For you, gradations in quality that most don't notice are the difference between ecstasy and indignity. Designing a menu for you is an agonizing task, so we'll offer up some precurated collections.

The Criterion Collection. *A trio of film lovers created this distribution company in 1984, and in the years since it has attained a near-religious status in the world of cinema. They pioneered many of the innovations that made it pleasant to watch movies at home, and when a movie cracks the Criterion, it's the cinematic equivalent of sainthood. And how does a film qualify? "We try not to be restrictive or snobby," the company explains. "All we ask is that each film in the collection be an exemplary film of its kind." Which means there are several Michael Bay titles in their catalogue.*

Luaka Bop. *David Byrne and Yale Evelev's record label was launched for exactly the reason a connoisseur shares anything: in the words of the Talking Heads frontman, "I wanted to turn friends on to stuff I liked." In 1988, that meant searching out obscure Brazilian psychedelia; nowadays it means bringing the New Jersey afropop of Delicate Steve to a wider audience. The unifying factor is excellent curation and a commitment to finding new sounds.*

NYRB Classics. *This publishing imprint of the New York Review of Books is dedicated to discovery. There are classics in translation, experimental works, memoirs, and cookbooks, all described as "the kind of books that people typically run into outside of the classroom and then remember for life." Especially admirable is their web form, on which anyone can request that they resurrect a classic that has unfairly gone out of print.*

Harmony in the Culture:
Building a Balanced Artwork

As a single work, what does cultural ketchup look like? What balances sweet, sour, salty, bitter, and umami in such a way that it has many imitators but no real competition? It might just be *Star Wars*.

Consider the balance:

- **Sweet:** A story of families separated and reunited, on both sides of the Force, working closely together, bickering, joking, talking to Ewoks, and ultimately triumphing.
- **Sour:** There are enough thrills to launch a thousand video games: lightsabers, lasers, dogfights, etc.
- **Salty:** Princess Leia as a prisoner in Jabba the Hutt's court. We derived salty from the entertainment preferences described as "dark"—as in the Dark Side.
- **Bitter:** Wagner, as we have seen. As well, Joseph Campbell's *The Hero with a Thousand Faces* has been cited by George Lucas as an inspiration. Campbell's 1949 book draws upon the work of Sigmund Freud and Carl Jung to examine the idea of the monomyth, the elemental story told across all cultures of a hero setting out on a fantastic journey. The idea that Lucas took this archetype to a galaxy far, far away and still made something that connected with

generations of moviegoers makes it seem like proof of concept: the theory put into action.

- **Umami:** The whole universe is as information-dense as anything in science fiction. When you consider how a minor character like Admiral Piett, one of several emotionless English apparatchiks of the Empire encountered in the first films, has spawned a cult following online (at www.piett.com; join and get exclusive access to their newsletter!), you can see how there are depths in these films that can be imagined even if they weren't intended.

There's no clearer proof that the original film (*Episode IV: A New Hope*) hit all the right notes than the fact that J. J. Abrams essentially remade it with the seventh (*Episode VII: The Force Awakens*), right down to the climactic mission to destroy the planet-sized warship—and no one seemed to mind. Compare that to George Lucas's prequels, which tried and failed to tell a complex new story about how democracies crumble (and weren't helped by a surfeit of abysmal dialogue and questionable CGI). You can't spike the bitterness of Heinz ketchup and still expect everyone to slather it on their fries.

Or consider the recipe for Lin-Manuel Miranda's *Hamilton*:

- **Sweet:** Alexander Hamilton is a "bastard, orphan, son of a whore and a Scotsman, dropped in the middle of a forgotten spot in the Caribbean" who finds success, fame, love, and his place in history. His romance with Eliza (and Angelica) is vivid, as is the story of their son. The Schuyler sisters have been compared to Destiny's Child.

- **Sour:** The rap battles are so thrilling, you forget they are eighteenth-century Cabinet meetings. Hamilton is woven through with rap and hip-hop history. Also, duels. And it's hard to be more rebellious than the American Revolution.
- **Salty:** Hamilton never knows when to stop. His confreres aren't above bragging about their exploits, on the battlefield as well as in the bedroom. And he invented the American political sex scandal.
- **Bitter:** "Who wants to go and see a show about America's first bureaucrat?" one of *Hamilton*'s producers asked rhetorically. Everyone, it turned out. The songs of *Hamilton* reference more music than seems possible, and yet they tie every genre together to tell a national story that overtly includes everyone.
- **Umami:** The musical is based on Ron Chernow's eight-hundred-page history of the first US Secretary of the Treasury, and Miranda made sure the details were as correct as they could be. "He tries first to stick to the facts, and if he has to deviate from the facts I have found that there is always a very good reason for him doing it," Chernow told the *New Yorker*.

The similarity between these two works is not just that they combine all the tastes in roughly equal measure, but that they draw these tastes from all over the culture. They are grand amalgams, drawing from many flavors and accentuating each by blending them in perfect harmony. You don't have to love what they do, but you should appreciate how they do it.

A TASTING MENU FOR THE NOSTALGIC

You are unashamedly hindsighted, perhaps for a bit of escapism, but more likely because you enjoy seeing how the classics permeate everything in the present day.

Eternal Sunshine of the Spotless Mind. The 2004 film represents a high point for both director Michel Gondry and writer Charlie Kaufman, who build a deeply felt romance that simultaneously looks forward, backward, and inward.

Remains of the Day. The 1989 novel by Kazuo Ishiguro is both a flawless re-creation of the end of an era and a devastating reminder of how easy it is to get wrapped up in our little worlds.

Stranger Things. Hey, remember the '80s? This Netflix series does, and the greatest trick it plays is telling a new story with all the familiar parts (and some of the familiar faces) of a distant decade.

Paris Trance. This 1998 novel by Geoff Dyer follows a young Englishman in the French capital who finds friends and a lover, builds a small but intense social life revolving around film, drugs, and sex, and then watches it fade away as quickly as it materialized.

Everyone's a Curator: Planning Your Cultural Meal

If you only watched, read, and listened to culture that ticked all the boxes, you would have plenty of spare time. The fact is, while harmony of tastes is deeply impressive in a single dish, more often we look to balance our meals, and beyond that, our diets. A burger for lunch may lead you to choose a salad for dinner.

It's not as though you consume a song, a book, a film, a painting, and a poem all in one sitting. Instead, it may be more helpful to examine your diet at regular intervals, checking the levels. Have there been one too many sitcoms on your Netflix queue? Do you really need another dense historical biography? If everything you watch is dark and edgy, wouldn't a touch of candy-colored sweetness make General Douglas MacArthur's hardscrabble childhood that much more salty?

But who has time to keep their cultural diet so exquisitely balanced? In the food world, if you need assistance in ensuring that you're eating the right foods in the ideal balance for optimum health, you consult a dietitian. In the cultural world, we call these sages curators.

Once a word applied only in museum galleries, "curator" has now become a commonplace identifier for anyone who sorts through the abundance of culture to find, present, and juxtapose the best bits in thoughtful and perhaps surprising ways. Which is basically everyone who has ever compiled a playlist.

As the *New York Times* reported in 2009, "among designers, disc jockeys, club promoters, bloggers and thrift-store owners, curate is code for 'I have a discerning eye and great taste.'" Since then, the word has become almost meaningless. (Doubling down on meaninglessness is the ubiquitous phrase "carefully curated," as though careless curation were even possible.)

We are now living in the late stages of what the perceptive art critic David Balzer calls Curationism, and in his 2014 book of the same name, he charts how we got here. It began with funding cuts and open hostility toward the arts in the 1980s, seen most clearly in the Reagan administration's battles to defund the National Endowment for the Arts. In response to less funding and more scrutiny, museums began to develop blockbuster exhibitions that used sophisticated marketing campaigns to bring in the crowds—and then made sure that they exited through the gift shop.

The economic necessity of selling more tickets coincided with the rise of identity politics, and as Balzer writes, "What better way to attract broader demographics than to show work pertaining to the exclusion of those very demographics?"

Central to all of this was the curator, "indispensable as agent, ambassador, organizer, facilitator, and provocateur." That gets us to curator as celebrity, which soon becomes celebrity as curator and results in exhibitions marketed by names like Miley Cyrus, Steve Martin, and Pharrell Williams.

(To curate the curator of curators: the best line in Balzer's book is directed at one of these celebrities, a musician whose footwear collaboration was allegedly inspired by her time on Mount Kilimanjaro: "Sometimes you have to climb a mountain to properly curate a sock.")

If everyone now curates in the general, pick-your-playlist sense of the term, what about in the more specific art-world meaning? If you let the people fill the museums, what would they choose?

A TASTING MENU FOR THE DABBLER

Art is long. Life is short. If you want to experience as much as you can, better keep it moving. You read three books at a time but won't hesitate to pull the chute if any of them start to drag. Why are you still reading this?

P. G. Wodehouse, any of the Jeeves stories. Part of the beauty of Wodehouse's work is that its beauty is uniformly distributed. Open a Jeeves novel to any page and you'll find Bertram Wooster in pitched battle against a cantankerous aunt, the sort who "chews broken bottles and kills rats with her teeth."

The Best American series of compilations. Published annually by Houghton Mifflin Harcourt, this series pretends to be definitive, as though the Best American Short Stories of 1996 were selected by science. But as the series has expanded to include comics, travel writing, infographics, and—usually the best one— nonrequired reading, it seems less an anachronism and more like a finishable, useful curation of all the writing out there.

The Economist *holiday double issue. Subscribing to* The Economist *is a commitment; picking up the annual Christmas double issue is a treat. The legendary British publication has a certain quirkiness about it all year round, but at the end of December the quirk takes over, resulting in stories about the history of Russian railways or the continuing reverberations throughout Paraguayan politics of the War of the Triple Alliance.*

Anyone's a Curator: The Problem of Too Many Cooks

In the 1990s, the Russian-born American art duo Komar and Melamid created a series of artworks they called the People's Choice. In eleven countries, they commissioned polling companies to find out exactly what people wanted to see in a painting. This exploration of "democracy and elitism by statistics" yielded, as you might expect, a series of bland works. In their own words, the artists "discovered that, regardless of sex, race, education, or income, in paintings, the majority of people preferred landscapes and the color blue."

The project was covered extensively around the world, and the artists maintained that they were merely using modern techniques to produce both the most- and least-wanted works. As Charles Mc-Grath wrote of a 2011 Melamid show in the *New York Times*, the artist is "by nature an ironist, so adept at serving as his own straight man that it's hard to tell how seriously he means to be taken. He may not know himself." The butt of the joke was not the polled but the pollsters. The questions they devised, apparently with minimal direction from the artists, were along the lines of "On the whole, would you say that you prefer seeing paintings of wild animals, like lions, giraffes, or deer, or that you prefer seeing paintings of domestic animals, like dogs, cats, or other pets?" (Wild animals were preferred in almost every country, save for Ukraine and Turkey.)

The project's underwhelming result can be easily explained through the Elements of Taste: they used a method that was all but guaranteed to elicit a popular, uncontroversial, and sweet response to create artwork in a format that succeeds when it is creative, dense, and bitter. It's like serving cotton candy to someone expecting rapini.

If you want to let the masses choose, you should at least give them a system that isn't built to fail. You need to give them an ideal filter, just as Francis Galton did when he asked them to guess the weight of an ox. What would such a system look like beyond the realm of livestock?

The answer can be seen in the Kreuzberg district of Berlin, where the Museum der Dinge—the Museum of Things—occupies the third floor of a tall building on a narrow street. It is formally the archive of the Deutscher Werkbund (German Work Federation), a collective of artists and manufacturers founded in 1907 to guide popular taste. The advent of the industrial revolution meant traditional craftsmen could be replaced by assembly lines. This is exactly the sort of transformation that led to the Luddite movement in England a century before, but in the best German tradition of cooperation, these naturally opposing camps were brought together to learn from one another.

They didn't always get along. In 1914, at the Werkbund's first great exhibition, two key members unveiled diametrically opposed philosophies for what they were all about.

Hermann Muthesius wanted an assembly line of impeccable work, and he issued a ten-point manifesto to that effect. "Standardization," he declared, "will alone make possible the development of a universally valid, unfailing good taste." And that good taste would restore a "universal significance which was characteristic of [architecture] in times of harmonious culture." And, not to put too fine a point on it, but the goods produced would be ideal for export, so it was vital to understand "the world will demand our products only when they are the vehicles of a convincing stylistic expression."

His fellow Werkbunder Henry van de Velde bristled at this idea of conformity, and so he countered with his own ten-point manifesto.

"So long as there are still artists in the Werkbund and so long as they exercise some influence on its destiny, they will protest against every suggestion for the establishment of a canon and for standardization," he wrote. "And it would be nothing short of castration to tie down this rich, many-sided, creative élan so soon." In his view, the artist was a "free spontaneous creator," and "nothing, nothing good and splendid, was ever created out of mere consideration for exports."

As you might expect, when the rigorous standardizers go to war with the freely spontaneous, the people who like planning tend to win the day. The Werkbund went the route of standardization, and similar organizations were established in Austria, Switzerland, and Great Britain. The Werkbund's mission was to ensure artists and manufacturers, merchants and consumers—the whole supply chain—worked tastefully together. This sounds ridiculously utopian, and the craziest part is that for a time, it seemed like they succeeded. As an American magazine declared in 1928, "those business men who think the only way to be successful is to sell merchandise of the poorest quality at the cheapest price, are not up to date any more."

The Werkbund is best known today for giving rise to the Bauhaus movement in architecture. And while both initially won favor with the Nazis—who saw the appeal of a centralized committee of tastemakers—that didn't last long. There were too many intellectuals involved, and the Bauhaus movement scattered in the 1930s while the Werkbund was closed in 1938.

In their efforts to promote good taste, the Werkbund had to define bad taste. One member in particular, Gustav Edmund Pazaurek, took this job on with gusto. He devised a criminal code of evil things, which was as comprehensive as it was judgmental. Some charges that he devised:

- "Decorative Brutality: When one of two decorative schemes not only disregards the other, but destroys it to usurp its place, that is brutality.
- "Bizarre Materials: Objects of human bone, skin, fingernails or hair; rhinoceros horns, ostrich eggs, shed antlers, animal teeth, vertebrae, feathers, fish scales; lizards, lobster claws, butterfly wings, beetle wings, live fireflies, egg membrane, cherry stones, spices, hazelnuts, straw, pine cones, mosses, tree fungus, cork, coloured sand, vegetables, sugar, butter, ice, bread, etc.
- "Unsuitable or Tricky Objects: Vessels that tip easily or cannot be cleaned; handles that can't be gripped; objects with sharp edges; also objects with overly fantastic or rich decoration at the expense of practical utility.
- "Functional Lies: Objects or parts which look deceptively useless or delicate, make false representations, or are superfluous, such as architectural ornamentation or decorative buttons.
- "Patent Humour: Useless, frivolous inventions; bad designs that concentrate attention on unimportant secondary purposes at the expense of the principal function."

Objects found in violation of Pazaurek's laws were locked up in a display case. He accumulated nearly a thousand items before tastes changed and the case was put into storage. It still belongs to the permanent collection of the Museum der Dinge.

The idea of a central committee that mandates a certain level of taste sounds bad for a number of reasons. Who are these elites? Why don't they trust the free market? And more specifically, why don't they trust you? All of which were actually better arguments in the early days of the Deutscher Werkbund than they are now.

If all taste is good and tastelessness only results when choices are made without thought, the best course of action for those who wish to improve the lowest common denominator is to gently but firmly make it slightly higher.

One way to see this in action is to shop for a front door for your house. When you head over to the local big-box hardware store, you'll find an aisle of front doors that violate many of Pazaurek's laws with their elaborate frosted windows, their gold trim, and their fake details. There's guaranteed to be one that's designed for a suburban version of Versailles.

And to be totally clear, that's fine. That's someone's idea of beauty, and in their specific context, it would work. But to sell it as one of a limited number of defaults is to ensure that it ends up on homes where it will look garish and out of place.

This is where the definition of taste we have arrived at faces its stiffest challenge: How are we to know the person who bought that door didn't put a great deal of thought into it? How do we know they settled? We don't, and we defer to them. But we also need to rerun the experiment with an elegant, unadorned door and see if that doesn't win the day. Only then, under these wildly improbable experimental conditions, would we be able to say the decision was made tastefully.

The ideal filter is almost impossible to impose, and that's probably for the best. The crowd may choose poorly, but Netflix doesn't let us share our accounts with the whole world. While everyone can choose, you don't have to listen to them. Remember the three words that define our times: you do you.

A TASTING MENU FOR THE ADVENTURER

For you, if it's not over-the-top, it doesn't register. Food should be packed with flavor. Like Beyoncé, you keep hot sauce in your purse. Bring it on.

Duel. *Steven Spielberg's first film, a 1971 made-for-TV drama, follows a showdown between "a man, a truck, and an open road." The director who would go on to send a legion of aliens, dinosaurs, and Nazis our way began with a simple premise that will terrify anyone who's ever been tailgated.*

Pulp Fiction. *When John Travolta stabbed Uma Thurman in the heart with an adrenaline-filled syringe, moviegoers were shocked, scandalized, and captivated. Tarantino's masterpiece had the same effect on the cinema of the 1990s.*

The Clock *by Christian Marclay. This twenty-four-hour art film is a minute-by-minute sampling of cinematic history that refers to the time of day. You see bits of movies and you can feel your brain trying to make a story of it all, though the only connections are the numbers on the clocks. It's utterly engrossing and hypnotic, the sort of movie that would make you lose all track of time if that weren't the entire subject.*

Someone's a Curator: The Genius of Diana Vreeland

The definition of "taste" we're using in this book—a conscious choice, neither good nor bad—has been the way of the fashion world forever. It explains the question that onlookers always ask when they see outlandish fashions on the runways of fashion shows: Who would ever wear that? The answer, of course, is nobody, or nobody except the glamorous models being paid to do so. It doesn't matter if you think it's good taste or bad taste—it just has to show some taste, and ideally be bitter enough to stand out from the crowd. Then it can be watered down and mass produced, so by the time the over-the-top five-star general's uniform gets to you, you barely notice that your new winter coat has epaulets.

Diana Vreeland, the legendary editor of *Vogue*, understood this.

If there was a time when good taste was one discrete set of preferences and bad taste another, it was before the twentieth century. After the First World War, with avant-garde art and music shocking genteel audiences across Europe, the boundaries began to blur. Vreeland came of age in the 1920s, and within these blurred boundaries. It was the age of "Make It New!" as the poet Ezra Pound famously ordered, and so it's no surprise that the first words of Vreeland's memoir are "I loathe nostalgia." She goes on to clarify that "I don't believe in anything before penicillin," which means her world started in 1928.

In that world, our definition of taste is the only one that matters. Vreeland captures this precisely with her description of her friend Elsie Mendl, perhaps the most famous interior decorator of the early twentieth century and someone who appreciated vulgarity:

Vulgarity is a very important ingredient in life. I'm a great be-
liever in vulgarity—if it's got vitality. A little bad taste is like
a nice splash of paprika. We all need a splash of bad taste—it's
hearty, it's healthy, it's physical. I think we could use more *of it.*
No *taste is what I'm against.*

Vreeland was very much in favor of her own tastes, broadcasting
them as indisputable facts. A smattering from *D.V.,* her 1984
stream-of-consciousness memoir:

- I don't like southern skies. To me
  they're not . . . enough.
- Lettuce is divine, although I'm not
  sure it's really food.
- Actually, I'm crazy about
  Indiana. So many people with
  style come from Indiana—not that I
  can give you a long list, but it's
  true.
- Have I told you that I think
  water is God's tranquilizer? Being
  part Scottish, I think to walk in the rain is
  just divine.
- I only believe in cremation—fast, fast cremation. Done with.

These bold assertions were nothing compared to the way she
made her name: not in saying what she liked, but rather giving
equally direct orders about what *you* should like.

Vreeland created a bizarro template for prescriptive fashion journalism with her "Why Don't You . . ." columns. Some of them read like useful suggestions; others like surreal thought experiments; most like dares to see just how gullible her readers were; and still others like the natural way you might end that insulting sentence (Get a job? Go play in traffic? Take a long walk off a short pier?).

"Why don't you . . . rinse your blond child's hair in dead champagne to keep it gold, as they do in France?" is likely her best known, probably because of the menace it evokes by placing the words "dead" and "child" so close to each other. It's also been pointed out that the French do no such thing, though of course the "they" in that sentence might specifically refer to only the most eccentric Parisians. Or it might be entirely fictional and thus part of the charm.

Other Why Don't Yous are more, shall we say, aspirational, like the suggestion to "have a private staircase from your bedroom to the library with a needlework carpet with notes of music worked on each step—the whole spelling your favorite tune?" And who among us wouldn't like to "give a new note to your sitting room by introducing a Victorian chair upholstered by Jensen in bright emerald green cotton, buttoned in white with little white chenille earrings on either side?"

And there are shades of Salvador Dalí in the idea that you ought to "embroider enormous red lobsters on a pure heavy silk tablecloth."

Were these suggestions self-parodying? It was impossible to tell, and that's what made them effective. In *D.V.*, Vreeland recalls that when she began at the magazine, she had a "brain wave"—to eliminate all handbags.

"It should all go into pockets," she proclaimed of her cigarettes, cosmetics, and cash. "Real pockets, like a man has, for goodness sake."

This brain wave led to the editor being summoned, and he was quick to explain the tiny flaw in Vreeland's logic: "Do you realize that our income from handbag advertising is God knows how many millions a year?"

It made sense, at that stage in her career, to let Vreeland air her possibly brilliant, perfectly impractical ideas in a venue where they would accentuate the advertisements, not drive them away. "Why don't you . . ." was the opposite of "You do you," and it worked. With her strong opinions and jaunty way of expressing them, Vreeland helped define American style, first at *Harper's Bazaar*, then as editor-in-chief at *Vogue*, and finally as a phenomenally successful consultant to the Costume Institute of the Metropolitan Museum of Art—in other words, a curator. Which is what she always was, really.

A TASTING MENU FOR THE MINIMALIST

More than a little is probably too much. You can taste a banquet in the first bite of food, and you probably meditate every morning. For you, just two books.

The Pigeon *by Patrick Suskind. This seventy-seven-page German novella follows Jonathan Noel, a fifty-three-year-old Parisian bank guard whose peaceful life is shattered when he finds a pigeon outside his front door. A bird flaps its wings and a man's existence is threatened.*

Don't Let the Pigeon Drive the Bus *by Mo Willems. This thirty-eight-page American children's book follows the Pigeon, who really wants to drive a bus. You, the reader, do not let him. The hero is a simply drawn bird with a simple goal, and in that he is a model of persistence and clarity.*

Something's a Curator: The Limits of Technology

On September 23, 1997, the Internet became a dramatically more interesting place to shop. It was on that date that Amazon—or Amazon.com, as it was then known—announced that it would group books by subject areas such as literary fiction and romance and introduce "the use of a proprietary technology, 1-Click ordering" that would eliminate "the need for customers to fill out order information every time they return to the site."

In hindsight, these two features bring to mind unwelcome visions of the horrible 1990s, when the only thing harder than finding a book online was filling out all the forms required to buy it. Bundled with these now-obvious innovations was the one that really lived up to the press release headline, "Amazon.com Catapults Electronic Commerce to Next Level with Powerful New Features." That was an "unrivaled state-of-the-art recommendation center," designed using the NetPerceptions GroupLens collaborative filtering technology. It marked the introduction of the "If You Like This Author" section, and in doing so used technology to offer some semblance of a digital rival to browsing.

Malcolm Gladwell wrote about collaborative filtering in the *New Yorker* in 1999, and he described it there as "a kind of doppelganger search engine," meaning that it would help you look for the things people exactly like you had already found. These words were published just a year after Google was founded, so at that point the idea of organizing the Internet by popularity was just emerging; what Gladwell called a doppelganger search engine would soon just be called a search engine. Parts of the article have the charming quality of assuming most of the future would be just like the present. For instance, Gladwell describes how a NetPerceptions executive envisions "a kiosk at your local video store where you could rate a dozen or so movies and have the computer generate recommendations for you from the movies the store has in stock." (Netflix had been founded two years earlier, but it had yet to enter the popular imagination.) The book business may change, Gladwell speculated, because "customers now have a way of narrowing down their choices to the point where browsing becomes easy again."

"Easy" may not be the exact word that comes to mind, but filtering certainly made browsing possible. What you lacked in the ability to scan the shelves and chat with the employees, you gained in the possibility of following "if you like this, you'll like that" chains to books you'd never heard of before. And in Gladwell's piece you can see the beginnings of *The Long Tail*, a 2006 book by Chris Anderson that (as its subtitle promised) explained "how endless choice is creating unlimited demand." The title refers to a bell-curve graph: the most popular products are at the peak of the curve, but as you slide down the side of the bell, you find the tail just keeps going and going. Niches are multiplying, and even the smallest areas of interest are now economically viable. Anderson identified three forces that helped create this long tail. The first is production (we're now making lots of different products, whether they're pop songs or potato chips); the second is distribution, which basically means the ability to sell on the Internet; and the third is filtering, or the way for people to figure out what it is they actually want. In other words, if you can make, store, and distribute cheaply, it makes economic sense to sell relatively unpopular products—so long as their customers can find them.

Anderson writes that "In a sense, good filters have the effect of driving demand down the tail by revealing goods and services that appeal more than the lowest common denominator fare that crowds the narrow channels of traditional mass-market distribution."

That's what a good filter ought to do on a macroeconomic level, but what should a good filter do for you? Ideally, it should be the perfect video store clerk, bookstore employee, and college radio DJ.

Imagine you could go into your favorite bookstore and stop time. Then you could methodically browse every single shelf, taking anything that looked remotely interesting—and a fair number of books that on first glance didn't appeal to you at all—back to a comfortable chair. And then, for as long as it took, you could browse the books one by one. You'd toss anything that didn't grab you, and form a neat pile of the things you really liked. Would it be exactly what you expected to enjoy, or would there be a smattering of unappealing books that, as the cliché goes, shouldn't have been judged by their covers? Either way, when we call time on the thought experiment, you have a reading list for the rest of your life.

That's how recommendation engines ought to work. Instead of stopping time, a program serves up exactly what you're going to like before you even know what it is.

But before you crack open the recommended book, you should

trust the recommender. A bookstore clerk has cultural authority; a sidebar on a website, less so. And so there's a formula these things follow: the engine should show you just enough things you already know you like to win your trust, and just enough things you know nothing about to convince you that it's worth your time. Beyond that, it should know when you're feeling adventurous and when you're looking for comfort—a much harder calculation, but the sort of thing Netflix can do by time of day.

So how does the filter work? There are three basic techniques, combinations of which you encounter all the time:

1. **The Usage-Based Filter.** This uses your past behavior to predict what you'll like next, and it works best if you've been rating everything on a star system. This is how Google guesses what you're going to search for next. But it suffers from what's called the cold start problem: you have to tell it what you like for it to tell you what people like you like. And who actually takes the time to go back and star review everything they've consumed? So maybe it just goes by your actual consumption—what you've read, watched, or listened to, but then it has no way to know if you actually enjoyed those works. Maybe you watched that dumb movie because you were exhausted and just needed to relax; maybe you bought that book for a friend; maybe you were streaming new music in the background.

2. **The Content-Based Filter.** This system measures how similar new books are to ones you already like. It's how the streaming service Pandora works. They call it the Music

Genome Project, and describe it thusly: "Each song in the Music Genome Project is analyzed using up to 450 distinct musical characteristics by a trained music analyst. These attributes capture not only the musical identity of a song, but also the many significant qualities that are relevant to understanding the musical preferences of listeners."

This is great in code but less so in reality, as it leads back to the problem Peter Rentfrow and his colleagues were trying to solve. First, how do you tag attributes? It's basically the same problem that the sociologists run into when they start slotting music into categories. If I liked *Fargo*, will it recommend movies with a strong female character, movies set in Minnesota, or movies by the Coen Brothers? What if I just really like the way snow looks on-screen? And second, if this system were fully implemented, it would become exceptionally hard to be an omnivore. It's all a bit too obvious, and doesn't really let the umami phenomena jump to the top of your feed.

3. **The Social-Based Filter.** This one is most interesting, and something that is legitimately new since Pierre Bourdieu did his polls and Malcolm Gladwell examined collaborative filtering. What do people you like like? This is basically the true advantage of the ideal bookstore clerk: you're obviously going to make a judgment of the person's character before trusting their recommendation, and you'll do that with countless social cues that no algorithm could hope to match. A friend, by this definition, is someone whose character you've already judged and found satisfactory. (That's maybe not something you'd put in a

greeting card, but it's true.) Until the rise of social
networks, most people didn't keep lists of their friends,
and they certainly didn't keep lists of their friends' friends.

All three of these filters exist today, but the social filter is by far the dominant force in guiding what we consume. It has created an age of micromanias, brief spasms of popular interest in specific bits of culture that seemingly came out of nowhere. It's the next stage of the long tail: niche culture of sufficient quality gets amplified by the network effect, and one day you look around and realize that everyone you know is listening to a podcast about a decade-old murder in Baltimore. As Willa Paskin observed, "The Internet's default mode is obsession."

This is at base the same crowd effect seen throughout history—and we react to it the same way. When tulips became a sensation in 1637 Holland, according to Charles Mackay, "nobles, citizens, farmers, mechanics, seamen, footmen, maidservants, even chimney sweeps and old clotheswomen, dabbled in tulips." And when Drake's "Hotline Bling" video became a sensation in 2015 web culture, it seemed like the same cross-section of society had strong opinions on whether the Canadian rapper's dance moves were terrific, horrific, or a clever way to stir up just that debate.

But while it's safe to say every Dutchman would have heard of tulipomania, it's possible that you blinked and missed "Hotline Bling." And therein lies the difference between the manias of history and the present era: with social media, we choose our own crowds. It's like a room full of people who were once attending the same concert but have now all discreetly slipped in earbuds to hear their own music. We still get the same communal feeling, but much less energy has gone into creating it. Because you've selected the crowd, you're much more likely to share their enthusiasm. But at the same time, that enthusiasm may well be something that barely registers in large pockets of mainstream culture.

This disconnect is everywhere. There's a bit of it in the Sarah Palin jab about the lamestream media, and the fact that of course national broadcasters can't accurately represent the millions of indi-

vidual outlooks of their viewers. That's why it can be startling when one of these micromanias bumps up against what everyone is watching, like when *Saturday Night Live* aired a parody of the podcast *Serial* in December 2014. They noticed our obsession!

And that in turn creates what Eli Pariser calls the filter bubble, and in his book of the same name, he warns that this autocuration creates "invisible autopropaganda, indoc-

trinating us with our own ideas, amplifying our desire for things that are familiar and leaving us oblivious to the dangers lurking in the dark territory of the unknown." The main focus of his argument is news, and rightly so: it's more worrisome if half the population thinks their leader is a demon than if, say, they think everyone loves bossa nova. (They do. They just don't know it yet.)

The good news is that, when it comes to helping us effectively sort through the infinite array of immediately available culture, the machines have failed.

A TASTING MENU FOR THE ENTHUSIAST

Why like when you can love? You are the opposite of the Dabbler. You are looking for something you can embrace so tightly, it becomes part of you. You don't just want to find a new thing; you want to find your new favorite thing. You want an author to name-drop in conversation, a director whose entire filmography you can binge-watch in a weekend, and a musician whose hooks will be your next ringtone. You'll go bitter if it means better.

> **The Inspector Maigret Omnibus** *by George Simenon. In twenty-eight short stories and seventy-five novels published from 1931 to 1972, Detective Chief Inspector Jules Maigret smokes a pipe and solves crimes. Many of the perpetrators are normal people who become obsessed with something and follow it to criminal ends. And then Maigret becomes obsessed with catching them. The consistent pairing of obsessions can easily become one.*

> **Found** *magazine. Davy Rothbart's magazine, website, podcast, musical, and life's work is as old as time: collecting ephemera other people have lost. A grainy photo of a bearded man holding a cat found on a Vienna sidewalk; a handwritten chart in which a young woman lists the pros and cons of her two suitors; countless angry notes left under windshield wipers. The only unifying theme is the obvious joy Rothbart takes when he receives these gems from around the globe.*

> **The Patrick Melrose Novels** *by Edward St. Aubyn. In four autobiographical novels, the author excavates a horrific childhood with bracing cleverness. Both therapeutic satire and satiric therapy.*

Look Around You. *You needn't have ever watched the dull science filmstrips this BBC series was parodying. The series of shorts, made in 2002 with a second batch in 2005 by Robert Popper and Peter Serafinowicz, stand alone in a world of eager students jotting down total nonsense in their copybooks.*

You're the Curator: Let's Do This

If so much data, money, and brainpower have been applied to this problem of what to like, why is the blank search box in the Spotify app so intimidating? Because the Internet as curator doesn't quite work. It can take every cue you offer, every action of the people like you, every characteristic of the things you used to like, and it can still feel like you're stuck. Ultimately, you are the curator. You have to make the first move.

In telecommunications, there is what's called the last-mile problem. It's easy enough to create a high-speed network, but wickedly difficult to run the cables from the street into your apartment. Elegant systems work perfectly until we get our grubby human hands on them.

This is the conclusion of Tom Vanderbilt's excellent 2016 book *You May Also Like: Taste in an Age of Endless Choice.* He debunks the utopian ideal of the long tail, noting that more options only make us seek out the most popular songs. The longer the tail, the more overwhelmed most of us become. He points out the many, many unconscious biases that sway our opinions, and just how fickle those opinions are. And he ends by suggesting that categorizing things, discussing how they are categorized, and considering how we developed our preferences for these categories is the key to explaining our taste. "The more interesting question is not *what* we like," Vanderbilt writes, "but *why* we like."

The Elements of Taste—the mapping of sweet, sour, salty, bitter, and umami onto all of culture—are an attempt at figuring out why.

Have you watched one too many salty dramas on premium cable? Maybe it's time to take up an umami hobby.

Have the sour thrills of pop-punk lost their edge? Perhaps some bitterly atonal experimental music will reawaken your taste buds.

Does your brain hurt from trying to figure all this out? Some sweet nothings may be just what you need.

But before you prescribe, you can describe. Examine what you watch, see, read, and hear. Make your own Tasting Note, perhaps using the template below. Start with things you love, hate, admire, and enjoy. Better yet, ask a friend about their favorite things, and diagnose their palate. (The measure of this method, and this entire book, may come when you next have to buy that friend a birthday present.)

Most of all, think about what it takes to make what you like. And then, when you have an inkling of what it is, flag the waiter down and order something you'll love.

TASTING NOTE ---- SUBJECT

COLOR/PATTERN

SWEET
SOUR
SALTY
BITTER
UMAMI

EXPLANATION:

☐ LOVE THIS! ☐ S'OK ☐ MEH ☐ THE WORST

ACKNOWLEDGMENTS

A smorgasbord of erudite and affable people shared their tasting notes throughout my writing of this book, and it only makes sense to sort them by the elements.

The Sweet Elite: *These gentle souls provided support and encouragement, both in ideas and logistics.* Jacob and Deborah Lazarovic. Patrick Bednarek and Katie Harper. Joshua Landy and Annie Williams, new friends whose new perspectives helped enormously. Greg Levey was helpful as only someone who knows the ropes can be. Joshy Errett and Samantha Grice. Jasmine Errett. Margo Varadi and Ariel Teplitsky. Jane Lazarovic and Brian Gillard. Ben Kaplan: All heart. And Becky Lazarovic, who purports to be salty, bitter, and umami but is obviously sweet in the best way.

Sour Rangers: *Because new ideas should be thrilling.* Greg Priestman's dedication to the works of Lee Child proves that. Tristan Zimmermann brings a sense of wonder and a commitment to cleverness to all he does. Agent/provocateur Sam Hiyate. Every Barry Hertz, sometimes.

Salty Dogs: *This cohort provides the necessary tang to both life and art.* Craig Courtice isn't afraid to go there, wherever "there" might be. (It might be Abu Dhabi.) Ryan Allen introduced me to the salty dog cocktail, a useful way to dispense of excess grapefruit juice. Jean Maxime Lachance proves a man can successfully be both philosopher and *The Muppet Show* in one lifetime.

Bitteratti: *This group helped broaden my cultural awareness, pointing me in new directions and offering a shove when needed.* The operatic arts could not hope for a better champion than James S. F. Wilson. David Lizoain is the guy who has this ongoing game wherein he jots down the horrible things people say after the word "but" in conversation. (As in, if someone says, "I don't want to sound like a Luddite, but . . .") J. Kelly Nestruck and Charlotte Corbeil-Coleman are perfectly paired, especially for the purposes of critique.

Umami Amigos: For their invaluable research assistance, Julie Bogdanowicz, Jess Whyte, and Nathalie Atkinson. Marian Lizzi, an amazing editor who has a knack for corralling ideas. Jason Chow is equally proficient in hair metal and French wines. For their astonishing ability to focus on both fine details and big pictures, Jessica Johnston and Steve Murray.

And finally, the harmonious Sarah Lazarovic, who ticks all the boxes.

REFERENCES

Aperitif

Gladwell, Malcolm. "The Ketchup Conundrum." *The New Yorker.* September 6, 2004.

Preoțiuc-Pietro, Daniel, Svitlana Volkova, Vasileios Lampos, Yoram Bachrach, and Nikolaos Aletras. "Studying user income through language, behaviour and affect in social media." *PloS ONE* 10, no. 9 (2015): e0138717.

Gifford, A. "History repeating [recorded by the Propellerheads featuring Shirley Bassey]." On *Decksandrumsandrockandroll.* London, England: Wall of Sound (1997).

Rentfrow, Peter J., Lewis R. Goldberg, and Daniel J. Levitin. "The structure of musical preferences: a five-factor model." *Journal of Personality and Social Psychology* 100, no. 6 (2011): 1139.

Rentfrow, Peter J., Lewis R. Goldberg, and Ran Zilca. "Listening, watching, and reading: the structure and correlates of entertainment preferences." *Journal of Personality* 79, no. 2 (2011): 223–58.

Landau, Mark J., Brian P. Meier, and Lucas A. Keefer. "A metaphor-enriched social cognition." *Psychological Bulletin* 136, no. 6 (2010): 1045.

Eskine, Kendall J., Natalie A. Kacinik, and Gregory D. Webster. "The bitter truth about morality: virtue, not vice, makes a bland beverage taste nice." *PloS ONE* 7, no. 7 (2012): e41159.

Gilead, Michael, Orian Gal, Marin Polak, and Yael Cholow. "The role of nature and nurture in conceptual metaphors." *Social Psychology* (2015).

Citron, Francesca M. M., and Adele E. Goldberg. "Metaphorical sentences are more emotionally engaging than their literal counterparts." *Journal of Cognitive Neuroscience* (2014).

Kordova, Shoshana. "word of the day: dugri: yes, that dress does make you look fat." *Haaretz*. August 20, 2014.

Palate Cleanser · The Ultimate Taste Test

Brillat-Savarin, Jean-Anthelme. *The Handbook of Dining, or, Corpulency and Leanness Scientifically Considered: Comprising the Art of Dining on Correct Principles Consistent with Easy Digestion, the Avoidance of Corpulency, and the Cure of Leanness; Together with Special Remarks on These Subjects.* Translated by L. F. Simpson. New York: Dappleton and Co., 1865.

Brillat-Savarin, Jean-Anthelme. *The Physiology of Taste, or Meditations on Transcendental Gastronomy.* Translated and edited by M.F.K. Fisher. New York: Vintage, 2009.

Fisher, Mary Frances Kennedy. *Serve It Forth.* New York: North Point Press, 1989.

Sweet

Granot, Elad, Thomas Brashear Alejandro, and La Toya M. Russell. "A socio-marketing analysis of the concept of cute and its consumer culture implications." *Journal of Consumer Culture* 14.1 (2014): 66–87.

Kinsella, Sharon. "Cuties in Japan." *Women, Media, and Consumption in Japan.* Honolulu: University of Hawaii Press, 1995: 220–54.

Okazaki, Manami, and Geoff Johnson. *Kawaii! Japan's Culture of Cute.* New York: Prestel, 2013.

Kuan, Cindy. "Cancer baby: cancer meets Kawaii culture." *The Lancet Oncology* 15 (July 2014): 796–97.

Yano, Christine R. "Wink on pink: interpreting Japanese cute as it grabs the global headlines." *The Journal of Asian Studies* 68, no. 3 (2009): 681–88.

Stasio, Marilyn. "Murder least foul: the cozy, soft-boiled mystery." *The New York Times*. October 18, 1992.

Foster, Jordan. "Some like it mild: cozy mystery." *Publishers Weekly*. May 4, 2009.

Watercutter, Angela. "My Little Pony corrals unlikely fanboys known as 'bronies.'" *WIRED*. June 9, 2011.

Steinberg, Neil. "When cuteness comes of age." *Mosaic Science* (July 19, 2016).

Fister, Barbara. "Profiling mystery readers." *Library Journal* (April 15, 2011).

Maloney, Jennifer. "In the world of cat fiction, fur flies over whether stars get speaking roles." *The Wall Street Journal*. February 26, 2016.

"'Bronies' galloping off with My Little Pony products." *License! Global* (November 2011): 18.

Robertson, Venetia Laura Delano. "Of ponies and men: *My Little Pony: Friendship is Magic* and the Brony fandom." *International Journal of Cultural Studies* (2013).

Snider, Brandon T. *My Little Pony: The Elements of Harmony: Friendship is Magic: The Official Guidebook*. New York: Little, Brown and Company, 2013.

Bissonnette, Zac. *The Great Beanie Baby Bubble: Mass Delusion and the Dark Side of Cute*. New York: Penguin Portfolio, 2015.

Wilson, Carl. *Let's Talk About Love: Why Other People Have Such Bad Taste*. New and Expanded Edition. New York: Bloomsbury, 2014. (orig. 2007).

Bonneville-Roussy, A., P. J. Rentfrow, M. K. Xu, and J. Potter. "Music through the ages: trends in musical engagement and preferences from adolescence through middle adulthood." *Journal of Personality and Social Psychology* 105, no. 4: 703.

Saunders, George. *Congratulations, by the Way: Some Thoughts on Kindness.* London: A & C Black, 2014.

Palate Cleanser • A Brief and Painless History of Taste

Bowie, David, Rick Wakeman, Terry Cox, Tim Renwick, Keith Christmas, Mick Wayne, Tony Visconti, Herbie Flowers, and Mick Woodmansey. *Space Oddity.* EMI, 1990.

Mitford, Nancy, ed. *Noblesse Oblige: An Enquiry into the Identifiable Characteristics of the English Aristocracy.* New York: Harper, 1956.

Woolf, Virginia. "Middlebrow" in *The Death of the Moth and Other Essays.* Vol. 294. Harcourt on Demand, 1974.

Lynes, Russell. *The Tastemakers: The Shaping of American Popular Taste.* Mineola, NY: Dover, 1980.

Bourdieu, Pierre. *Distinction: A Social Critique of the Judgement of Taste.* Cambridge, MA: Harvard University Press, 1984.

Friedland, Roger. "The endless fields of Pierre Bourdieu." *Organization* 16, no. 6 (2009): 887–917.

Bennett, T., M. Emmison, and J. Frow. *Accounting for Tastes: Australian Everyday Cultures.* Melbourne: Cambridge University Press, 1999.

Robette, Nicolas, and Olivier Roueff. "An eclectic eclecticism: methodological and theoretical issues about the quantification of cultural omnivorism." *Poetics* 47 (2014): 23–40.

Sour

Liem, Djin Gie, and Julie A. Mennella. "Heightened sour preferences during childhood." *Chemical Senses* 28.2 (2003): 173–80.

Charles Darwin. "A biographical sketch of an infant." *Mind* 2, no. 7 (1877): 285–94.

Frauenfelder, Mark. "Gross National Product." *WIRED*. June 1, 1999.

Kildegaard, Heidi, Erik Tønning, and Anette K. Thybo. "Preference, liking and wanting for beverages in children aged 9–14 years: role of sourness perception, chemical composition and background variables." *Food Quality and Preference* 22.7 (2011): 620–27.

Beecher, Louise. "Drug images sell candy, worry adults." *Hartford Courant*. November 10, 1997.

May, Cybele, and Maria Smith. "Episode 31: Sour Power." *Candyology 101* via Candyblog.net. Podcast audio. February 17, 2016.

SLOCHE Case. "Cassies 2002 Cases. Brand: Sloche. Advertiser: Alimentation Couche-Tard Inc. Agency: Beauchesne, Ostiguy et Simard. Winner: Best Launch Gold. Retail Silver." Accessed March 13, 2017. http://cassies.ca/content/caselibrary/winners/02_SLOCHE.pdf.

"Gross-out strategy works for Couche-Tard's 'Sloche.'" *Strategy*. July 2, 2001.

Musgrave, Sarah. "Lipo: a flavour only a kid could love." *Montreal Gazette*. October 21, 2006.

Rakonowchuk, Peter. "Clown calls for protest of ads with clown being hacked to pieces." *The Canadian Press*. May 7, 2009.

"Un changement stratégique pour Sloche, produit-vedette de Couche-Tard." *Infopresse*. May 25, 2015.

Reidelbach, Maria. *Completely MAD: A History of the Comic Book and Magazine.* New York: Little, Brown and Company, 1991.

Jayasena, Vijay, and Ian Cameron. "Brix/acid ratio as a predictor of consumer acceptability of crimson seedless table grapes." *Journal of Food Quality* 31.6 (2008): 736–50.

Sharrock, Justine. "Office role-play? Meet the people who pretend to work at an office together." *Fast Company.* October 9, 2014.

Marcus, Greil. *Lipstick Traces: A Secret History of the Twentieth Century.* Cambridge, MA: Harvard University Press, 1989.

Palate Cleanser • The Wisdom and Foolishness of Crowds

Mackay, Charles. *Memoirs of Extraordinary Popular Delusions and the Madness of Crowds.* London: George Routledge and Sons, 1869.

Galton, Francis. "Vox populi (the wisdom of crowds)." *Nature* 75, no. 7 (1907): 450–51.

Lanier, Jaron. *You Are Not a Gadget.* New York: Vintage, 2010.

Salty

Zimmer, Ben. "A 'salty' word with a promising future." *The Wall Street Journal.* January 16, 2015.

Keast, Russell S. J., and Paul A. S. Breslin. "An overview of binary taste–taste interactions." *Food Quality and Preference* 14.2 (2003): 111–24.

Sharkey, Betsy. "Nasty boys (and girls): beyond the big bland-out; the 'new vulgarity' is seeping into advertising." *Adweek Eastern Edition* (June 18, 1990): 44.

Dahl, Steve. "Descent into the Archives—July 12, 2014." This thirty-fifth Anniversary DD show sketches out the history of Disco Demolition. Podcast episode. Steve Dahl Network. www.dahl.com/descent-into-the -archives/podcast/descent-into-the-archives-7-12-2014/.

Frank, Gillian. "Discophobia: antigay prejudice and the 1979 backlash against disco." *Journal of the History of Sexuality* 16, no. 2 (2007): 276–306.

Gaar, Gillian G. "Disco demolition marks 35th anniversary." *Goldmine*. September 2014.

Seabrook, John. *The Song Machine: Inside the Hit Factory*. New York: W. W. Norton & Co., 2015.

Leiby, Richard. "'My Sharona,' revealing a knack for current affairs?" *The Washington Post*. April 17, 2005.

Lawrence, Tim. *Love Saves the Day: A History of American Dance Music Culture, 1970–1979*. Durham, NC: Duke University Press, 2003.

Edwards, Gavin. *Is "Tiny Dancer" Really Elton's Little John?: Music's Most Enduring Mysteries, Myths, and Rumors Revealed*. New York: Three Rivers Press, 2010.

Lawson, Nigella. "My Love Affair with Salted Caramel." *Stylist*, issue 105. December 7, 2011.

Palate Cleanser · The Impossibility of Bad Taste

Jacobellis v. Ohio. 378 US 184, 84 S. Ct. 1676, 12 L. Ed. 2d 793 (1964).

Gewirtz, Paul. "On 'I know it when I see it.'" *The Yale Law Journal* 105, no. 4 (1996): 1023–47.

Stern, Jane, and Michael Stern. *The Encyclopedia of Bad Taste*. New York: HarperCollins Publishers, 1991.

Andersen, Kurt. "You say you want a devolution?" *Vanity Fair*. January 2012.

Bitter

Lee, M. Owen. *Wagner's Ring: Turning the Sky Round.* New York: Limelight Editions, 1998.

McLagan, Jennifer. *Bitter.* Toronto: HarperCollins Canada, 2014.

Chen, Bin-Bin, and Lei Chang. "Bitter struggle for survival: evolved bitterness embodiment of survival motivation." *Journal of Experimental Social Psychology* 48.2 (2012): 579–82.

Skeie, Trish R. "Norway and coffee." *The Flamekeeper: Newsletter of the Roasters Guild.* Spring 2003.

Manzo, John. "Coffee, connoisseurship, and an ethnomethodologically informed sociology of taste." *Human Studies* 33.2–3 (2010): 141–55.

Toro-González, Daniel, Jill J. McCluskey, and Ron C. Mittelhammer. "Beer snobs do exist: estimation of beer demand by type." *Journal of Agricultural and Resource Economics* 39, no. 2 (2014): 174–187.

Sagioglou, Christina, and Tobias Greitemeyer. "Bitter taste causes hostility." *Personality and Social Psychology Bulletin* 40, no. 12 (2014): 1589–97.

Bilger, Burkhard. "A better brew: the rise of extreme beer." *The New Yorker.* November 24, 2008.

Bosson, Jennifer, Amber B. Johnson, Kate Niederhoffer, and William B. Swann Jr. "Interpersonal chemistry through negativity: bonding by sharing negative attitudes toward others." *Personal Relationships* 13 (2006): 135–50.

Kois, Dan. "Eating your cultural vegetables." Riff. *The New York Times Magazine.* April 29, 2011.

Dargis, Manohla, and A. O. Scott. "In defense of the slow and the boring." *The New York Times.* June 3, 2011.

Kapferer, Jean-Noël, Cindy Klippert, and Lara Leproux. "Does luxury have a minimum price? An exploratory study into consumers' psychology of luxury prices." *HAL* (2014).

Schwartz, Barry. *The Paradox of Choice: Why More Is Less—How the Culture of Abundance Robs Us of Satisfaction*. New York: HarperCollins, 2005.

Andreeva, Nellie. "HBO drama pilot *The Corrections* not going forward." *Deadline Hollywood*. May 1, 2012.

Chayka, Kyle. "Welcome to AirSpace: how Silicon Valley helps spread the same sterile aesthetic across the world." *The Verge*. August 3, 2016.

Gopnik, Blake. "Fighting bad taste from within." *The New York Times*. March 27, 2016.

Palate Cleanser · The Myth of Supertasters

Fox, Arthur L. "The relationship between chemical constitution and taste." *Proceedings of the National Academy of Sciences of the United States of America* 18.1 (1932): 115–20.

Blakeslee, Albert F. "Genetics of sensory thresholds: taste for phenyl thio carbamide." *Proceedings of the National Academy of Sciences of the United States of America* 18.1 (1932): 120–30.

Bartoshuk, L. M., V. B. Duffy, and I. J. Miller. "PTC/PROP tasting: anatomy, psychophysics, and sex effects." *Physiology & Behavior* 56.6 (1994): 1165–71.

Bohannon, John. "A taste for controversy. profile: Linda Bartoshuk." *Science* 328 (June 18, 2010).

Hayes, John E., and Russell S. J. Keast. "Two decades of supertasting: where do we stand?" *Physiology & Behavior* 104.5 (2011): 1072–1074.

Umami

Nakamura, Eiichi. "One hundred years since the discovery of the 'umami' taste from seaweed broth by Kikunae Ikeda, who transcended his time." *Chemistry—An Asian Journal* 6, no. 7 (2011): 1659–63.

Koseki, Kelichi. "Marketing strategies as adopted by Ajinomoto in Southeast Asia." *Journal of Advertising Research* 30, no. 2 (1990): 31–34.

Stuckey, Barb. *Taste What You're Missing: The Passionate Eater's Guide to Why Good Food Tastes Good*. New York: Free Press, 2012.

Bartlett, Tom. "A Norse God among the lit critters." *The Chronicle of Higher Education*. February 14, 2016.

Davis, Lydia. "Freelance." *The Times Literary Supplement*. February 28, 2014.

Dillon, Kathleen M. "Popping sealed air capsules to reduce stress." *Psychological Reports* 71, no. 1 (1992): 243–46.

Vanderbilt, Tom. "This bland is my bland." *Interiors* 160, no. 2 (February 2001): 59.

Dyer, Geoff. "Martin Parr's small world" in *Working the Room: Essays*. Edinburgh, Scotland: Canongate, 2015.

Aspden, Peter. "Lunch with the FT: Martin Parr." *Financial Times*. February 16, 2007.

Mlotek, Haley. "Why the *Gilmore Girls* fandom lives on." *The New York Times Magazine*. July 13, 2015.

Oxley, Andy. *Born to be Mild*. Documentary. Screen 3 Productions, 2015.

Kottke, Jason. "Born to be Mild: The Dull Men's Club." Kottke.org. September 30, 2016.

Cohen, Randy. "Elegy for the hobby." *The New York Times Magazine*. May 25, 1997.

Ross, Deborah. "Please let us women join the Dull Men's Club too." *The Times of London.* October 1, 2015.

Gelber, Steven M. *Hobbies: Leisure and the Culture of Work in America.* New York: Columbia University Press, 1999.

Baab-Muguira, Catherine. "Millennials are obsessed with side hustles because they're all we've got." *Quartz.* June 23, 2016.

Palate Cleanser · Aging Tastefully

Methven, Lisa, Victoria J. Allen, Caroline A. Withers, and Margot A. Gosney. "Aging and taste." *Proceedings of the Nutrition Society* 71, no. 04 (2012): 556–65.

Boyce, J. M., and G. R. Shone. "Effects of ageing on smell and taste." *Postgraduate Medical Journal* 82.966 (2006): 239–41.

Mojet, Jos, Elly Christ-Hazelhof, and Johannes Heidema. "Taste perception with age: generic or specific losses in threshold sensitivity to the five basic tastes?" *Chemical Senses* 26, no. 7 (2001): 845–60.

Auden, Wystan Hugh. "Reading: an essay" in *The Dyer's Hand and Other Essays.* New York: Vintage, 1989.

Larkin, Philip. "What's become of Wystan?" *The Spectator.* July 14, 1960. 24.

Harmony

McGee, Harold. *On Food and Cooking: The Science and Lore of the Kitchen.* New York: Simon & Schuster, 2007.

Mead, Rebecca. "All about the Hamiltons." *The New Yorker.* February 9, 2015.

Chang, David. "The unified theory of deliciousness." *WIRED.* July 19, 2016.

Williams, Alex. "On the tip of creative tongues." *The New York Times*. October 2, 2009.

Balzer, David. *Curationism: How Curating Took over the Creative World and Everything Else*. Toronto: Coach House Books, 2014.

"Komar & Melamid: The Most Wanted Paintings on the Web." Dia Center for the Arts. http://awp.diaart.org/km/.

Conrads, Ulrich. *Programs and Manifestoes on 20th-century Architecture*. Cambridge, MA: MIT Press, 1970.

Mihalik, Julius. "Meeting of the Deutscher Werkbund, Munich, 1928." *The American Magazine of Art* 19, no. 9 (September 1928): 526–27.

Vreeland, Diana. *D.V.* Edited by George Plimpton and Christopher Hemphill. New York: Alfred A. Knopf, 1984.

Pérez, Luis G., Beatriz Montes-Berges, and Maria del Rosario Castillo-Mayen. "Boosting social networks in Social Network–Based Recommender System." In *Intelligent Systems Design and Applications (ISDA)*, 11th International Conference. IEEE (2011): 426–31.

Paskin, Willa. "Totally obsessed: the new age of cultural manias." *Slate*. November 30, 2014.

Vanderbilt, Tom. *You May Also Like: Taste in an Age of Endless Choice*. New York: Alfred A. Knopf, 2016.

Vanderbilt, Tom. "The science behind the Netflix algorithms that decide what you'll watch next." *WIRED*. August 7, 2013. http://www.wired.com/2013/08/qq_netflix-algorithm/.

INDEX

ABOUT THE AUTHOR

Benjamin Errett spent a decade editing the arts pages of the *National Post*. Once they were finally edited, he wrote this book. Recommended pairings include *Elements of Wit*, his previous book, and a dry white wine. Maybe a Sémillon? He dips his fries in mayonnaise and lives in Toronto.